A Guide to Successful
Meeting Planning

A Guide to Successful Meeting Planning

Suzanne Stewart Weissinger
Fleet Business School
Annapolis, Maryland

John Wiley & Sons, Inc.
New York   Chichester   Brisbane   Toronto   Singapore

*Recognizing the importance of preserving what has been written, it is a policy of John Wiley &
Sons, Inc., to have books of enduring value published in the United States printed on acid-free
paper, and we exert our best efforts to that end.*

This publication is designed to provide accurate and authoritative information in regard to the
subject matter covered. It is sold with the understanding that the publisher is not engaged in
rendering legal, accounting, or other professional service. If legal advice or other expert
assistance is required, the services of a competent professional person should be sought.
FROM A DECLARATION OF PRINCIPLES JOINTLY ADOPTED BY A COMMITTEE OF THE
AMERICAN BAR ASSOCIATION AND A COMMITTEE OF PUBLISHERS.

Library of Congress Cataloging-in-Publication Data

Weissinger, Suzanne Stewart.
  A guide to successful meeting planning / Suzanne
Stewart Weissinger.
    p. cm.
  Includes index.
  ISBN 0-471-54523-6
    1. Meetings—Planning—Handbooks, manuals, etc. I. Title.
HF5734.5.W45 1992
  658.4'56—dc20   91-10133

Printed in the United States of America
10 9 8 7 6 5 4 3 2 1

Preface

No matter what your occupation, you will at some time plan a meeting. Maybe it is:

- ❑ Thanksgiving dinner;
- ❑ a garden club luncheon;
- ❑ a monthly office staff meeting;
- ❑ a Jaycees business meeting;
- ❑ a banquet for the retiring CEO;
- ❑ a fund-raiser for a charitable organization;
- ❑ a regional sales training seminar; or
- ❑ an annual conference involving hundreds of participants.

This book helps you to plan a meeting—an undertaking that is basically a chaotic activity. From the idea to hold a meeting to the sound of the closing gavel, you will find information, instructions, and examples to lead you along and checklists to help you define what needs to be done and remind you of details you might have forgotten.

The scope of meeting planning touches all areas of the travel industry. Professionals and students in all tourism occupations—transportation, accommodations, food service, destinations, travel agencies, and wholesalers—will find that learning about meeting planning activities melds all segments of the travel industry together.

Planning a meeting is like sitting before a jigsaw puzzle with hundreds of pieces spread out. You know what the picture is supposed to look like, but where to start? Suddenly one piece looks as if it fits into another. Yes! Then another fits, and another. Some of the pieces you lay aside, knowing that eventually they will connect to the total scene. There is no method, no pattern, as you slowly place and fit each piece. You have to put all of the parts together for the puzzle to be solved.

Meeting planning is carefully placing one puzzle piece at a time, tying one action to another, searching for two pieces that fit, performing isolated activities that eventually become a part of the whole. In one day you may sign a contract with the audiovisual supplier, process 50 registrations, and negotiate a hosted luncheon. There is no pattern, yet each separate activity is dependent on the whole. A great feeling of satisfaction comes when all activities connect to make a complete picture—a successful meeting.

How to Use This Book

A fabled one-page communications test begins "Read the entire page." Most people ignore that first direction and begin laboriously writing the answer to each question. The last line states, "Do not write on this paper." The directions for the use of this book are "First read the entire book," because planning a meeting involves building blocks of interdependent tasks.

Chapter 1 describes meeting planning as a profession: what types of skills and personality traits are common to successful meeting planners and what meeting planners do. A master timetable schedules the various planning tasks. Chapters 2 and 3 describe why people meet and the many different types of meetings. Chapter 4 leads the meeting planner or meeting organizer through the steps of program planning. The timing, type of sessions, and other activities must be decided upon before choosing a meeting site.

Chapters 5 and 6 define what criteria are important in choosing the best location and property for the meeting. Marketing the meeting is covered in Chapter 7, and producing the materials needed for the meeting is treated in Chapter 8.

Chapter 9 tells how to manage reservations and registrations. Chapter 10 and Chapter 11 explore planning and on-site activities concerning food and beverage and organizing the meeting sessions. Chapter 12 discusses transportation and free-time activities.

Certain terms are used interchangeably throughout this book. Most often the terms *convention* and *conference* are used generically. Another example of synonymous terms are *hotel*, *motel*, and *motor inn*. The term *hotel* is often used to denote any one of several types of properties.

The Chapter Objectives outline learning goals, and the Chapter Activities help you practice meeting planning skills. You can adapt the chapter activities to an actual meeting or apply them to the sample meetings outlined. Checklists and evaluations are provided throughout the book.

Ready, Set, Go!

The meeting business is exciting. Managing a meeting is hard work, but rewarding. It is task-oriented. Results are visible, tangible, and measurable, and satisfaction is immediate. With the help of this book, you can complete your next meeting planning puzzle moves quickly, efficiently, and with more confidence.

Pay attention to those details, expect the unexpected, plan for contingencies, and organize, organize, organize, UNTIL WE MEET AGAIN.

Contents

Checklists

A Guide to Successful Meeting Planning

1

Are You a Meeting Planner?

**Upon completion of this chapter,
you will be able to:**

1. Identify what skills meeting planners use
2. Know the ideal personality traits of a meeting planner
3. Understand the scope of tasks involved in meeting planning

> WANTED: Highly organized, detail-oriented individual with excellent ability to work with and manage others. Must have training or experience in social behaviorism, advertising, printing, budgeting, travel arrangements, theater, electrical engineering, law, culinary arts, and computers. The ideal candidate will be exceptionally motivated and work well under extreme pressure. Willing to work 14-hour days.

Who is this talented person that the classified ad seeks? It might be you, if you are in charge of a meeting. Meeting planners come from a variety of social and academic backgrounds, employment experiences, managerial environments, and income levels. They demonstrate multiple skills and varied abilities.

The meeting planner might be the program chair for a social organization. Often the first vice-president of a club acts as program chair and is in charge of securing speakers, choosing a site and the menu, and registering participants at the club's weekly, monthly, or annual meetings.

The person who speaks up and says, "Oh, why don't we hold next year's meeting in my hometown, Cityville. It's so nice," might become the meeting planner. Perhaps the meeting planner is the secretary whose boss passes by and says, "I need to meet with the state distributors next week. Contact them. Find us a hotel, reserve a meeting room, make their reservations . . . you know, set it up."

Management often equates travel planning with meeting planning and assigns meeting planning duties to the corporate travel office. Instead of processing travel orders and reimbursement claims, those employees find themselves responsible for designing a meeting. Likewise, a travel agent who handles personal and business travel might be approached to orchestrate a meeting.

Today meeting planning is a profession in its own right. There are more than 200,000 full-time and part-time meeting planners in the United States. Sometimes a meeting planner's job duties may include advertising, public relations, and sales, but more and more meeting planning stands alone as a job description and is no longer just an adjunct duty for someone whose time is primarily devoted to other activities.

Many associations and corporations now have meeting planners on their staffs. An organization that holds several conferences each year may employ a meeting planner or meeting manager who plans and executes all meetings. There are also independent meeting planners who work on a consulting basis, planning meetings for several different organizations.

The professional status that is now being accorded to meeting planners is due to the establishment of several organizations. Meeting Planners International was founded in 1972 and holds training and information exchange programs. The Convention Liaison Council established a Certified Meeting Professional examination, which gives professional prestige to those who pass it. The Professional Convention Management Association has designed a model curriculum for colleges and universities that offer meeting management courses and acts as the accrediting agency for such programs.

There are many other associations for meeting and exhibit planners. The Association of Independent Meeting Planners, Foundation for International Meetings, International Exhibitors Association, National Society of Sales Training Executives, and Society of Company Meeting Planners are but a few. See Appendix C for a complete listing of meeting planning organizations.

The recognition of meeting planning as a profession continues to grow. The sophistication of today's technology and the increasing awareness of human behavior make meeting planning more complex. People are beginning to recognize meeting planning as a skill and an art that takes training and practice.

What Does a Meeting Planner Do?

Re-read the classified ad at the beginning of this chapter. The person sought must have many skills and much experience. Many of the tasks involved in meeting planning demand personal knowledge while others require a thorough knowledge of available resources. The text below summarizes a few of these tasks.

A meeting planner may collaborate with senior management to plan the content of a program, in which case the planner needs to understand the subject matter to be presented at the meeting. Someone with a business degree probably could not help plan the program content for a meeting of a foundation for respiratory research; in a case like this, the planner might handle only the logistics of the meeting. No matter what the subject of the meeting, however, a planner can ask questions and guide meeting organizers in establishing goals, aims, and objectives for the meeting.

A meeting planner will also have to understand human behavior. A planner may advise on the optimal timing and pacing of a program based on his or her knowledge of average attention spans and how often refreshment breaks are needed.

A meeting planner also researches things such as past meeting history and participant profiles. If such information is not available, the planner must act as an investigative reporter to compile this information. Possible sites and properties for the meeting must be researched and investigated. A knowledge of geography and the accommodations industry is needed.

Budgeting is a major part of meeting planning. Keeping expenditures within set limits requires constant monitoring. Exploring costs, taking bids, and reconciling statements is tedious yet vital work. The meeting planner prices registration and might be called on to solicit donations or sponsors to defray the costs of the meeting. The planner also counts and recounts the number of attendees, rooms reserved, and meals to order.

Contracts are negotiated with any number of organizations when arranging a meeting and require close attention on the part of the planner.

The property contract is extremely detailed. Transportation, audiovisual, technical, catering, attraction, and event companies are but a few of the outside vendors that will demand written contractual agreements for providing services for the meeting.

Planners also promote their meetings and need to know about advertising, promotion, and public relations. The psychological appeal of a meeting must be assessed in order to effectively promote it. Printed material, both for promotional purposes and for distribution at the meeting, must be assembled. The planner must thus understand the intricacies of printing.

Setting the stage for the meeting is a primary duty of the planner. The audience seating arrangements, head table, audiovisual equipment needs, entertainment, and decor must all be staged, and exhibits must be managed. And, meeting staff must be trained. On-site materials must be organized. To this end, the planner must have excellent managerial and personnel skills.

Although computerized records management is available, tracking reservations and registration is ultimately the responsibility of the meeting planner, who must be familiar with records management software and its applications.

For many meetings, the planner acts as travel agent or tour guide. The planner may arrange travel for presenters and for attendees. Extracurricular activities, entertainment, and recreation may also be the responsibility of the planner.

Following is a checklist of 20 functions that a meeting planner might be called upon to perform. Some meetings will require all of these functions; others, only a few. As a first step in planning any meeting, determine which of these duties are required of you.

MEETING PLANNING TASK CHECKLIST

1. Set meeting objectives, goals, and aims.

2. Profile the typical participant.

3. Advise on or establish the program content.

4. Initiate the budget.

5. Select the site for the meeting.

6. Choose the facilities for the meeting.

7. Coordinate the meeting arrangements with the convention services manager.

8. Plan and direct food and beverage.

9. Arrange transportation.

10. Organize entertainment and recreation.

11. Plan companion programs.

12. Develop exhibits.

13. Negotiate contracts.

14. Set registration costs.

15. Produce printed materials.

16. Arrange marketing and publicity.

17. Manage reservations and registrations.

18. Design function room setup.

19. Train staff.

20. Evaluate the meeting.

Each meeting has its own pace and scheduling. A planner may be present when the idea for the meeting is first discussed or may be stepping in only three months prior to a meeting that is already somewhat organized.

The pace quickens as the meeting time approaches. It's impossible to describe the frantic activity two weeks before a meeting. The planner will most likely spend the majority of the time on the phone, trouble-shooting and putting out fires. Eight-hour days become 12 hours long, and no meeting planner can escape waking in the middle of the night to scribble additions to the list of things to remember.

The sample meeting planning timetable shown in Figure 1.1 puts the planning activities into perspective and further shows the complexity of a meeting planner's job. The timetable acts as a master checklist for a large national meeting. Many activities require individual checklists which are provided throughout this book.

For each of the activities shown, the meeting planner acts as communicator and manager. Without communication and managerial skills, failure is almost guaranteed.

Who Makes a Good Meeting Planner?

PERSONAL: Seeking likable people-person who can communicate with me. Must be very organized, have sense of humor, flexibility, and lots of energy. Must know good food and entertainment and be willing to stay up late.

In the personal ads, people are always searching for the ideal companion. A meeting planner must also combine many of these dream qualities.

Meeting planners must be good communicators. Some meeting planners work closely with senior management, talking with CEOs and establishing management policies and positions. But meeting planners must also be able to communicate with electricians and housekeepers.

Planners must be people-oriented and outgoing yet tactful and polite.

MEETING PLANNING TIMETABLE

Time
Before
Meeting   **Meeting Planning Activity**

2–5 years
- ❑ Define objectives
- ❑ Set length of meeting and desired dates
- ❑ Estimate attendance
- ❑ Profile attendees
- ❑ Pick site
- ❑ Choose and sign contract with meeting property
- ❑ Establish rough budget and registration fee
- ❑ Contact funding sources
- ❑ Print meeting stationery

12 months
- ❑ Formulate agenda (subjects, presentors, timing)
- ❑ Invite presentors and dignitaries
- ❑ Assign session chairs and escorts
- ❑ Contract with paid speakers
- ❑ Formulate checklists
- ❑ Contract with official airline, travel agency, and car rental companies
- ❑ Design marketing materials (including tentative program)
- ❑ Sell exhibit space
- ❑ Sell program advertising space
- ❑ Contact potential sponsors/hosts
- ❑ Make tentative contracts with audiovisual equipment companies, ground transportation services, and recreation, entertainment, and tour operators
- ❑ Confirm Convention and Visitors Bureau (CVB) contribution
- ❑ Complete budget

10 months
- ❑ Check exhibit, advertising, and sponsor sales
- ❑ Order giveaways
- ❑ Seek mailing lists
- ❑ Buy trade media advertising space (schedule 3–6 months prior to meeting)
- ❑ Establish credit and payment policies with meeting property

6 months
- ❑ Formulate registration policies and procedures
- ❑ Establish registration database
- ❑ Finalize marketing material artwork
- ❑ Get bids from printers

Figure 1.1 **Meeting Planning Timetable**

Time Before Meeting	Meeting Planning Activity
6 months (*continued*)	❑ Design and send media advertising artwork ❑ Send news releases to interested media ❑ Sign contracts with ground transportation, audiovisual suppliers, tour operators, entertainment, decorators, and other outside contractors
4 months	❑ Obtain flyers from hotel, CVB, airline, travel agency, car rental company ❑ Reconfirm with CVB if providing personnel ❑ Mail marketing materials ❑ Purchase nametag holders ❑ Design and print nametags ❑ Establish procedures for nametag completion ❑ Send tape/proceedings release, transportation requests forms to audiovisual suppliers and presenters ❑ Obtain artwork from program advertisers ❑ Arrange with restaurants if dine-around to be held ❑ Contract with caterer ❑ Contract with photographer
3 months	❑ Begin processing registrations, sending confirmations and invoices, and systematically preparing nametags ❑ Begin telemarketing ❑ Design and order printed meeting materials such as signs, tickets, folders, and vouchers ❑ Make presenters' travel reservations and send them confirmations ❑ Name VIP escorts ❑ Choose menus ❑ Send function sheets to hotel ❑ Confirm all contracts ❑ Buy decorations ❑ Send audiovisual contractor the presenters' requirements ❑ Begin checking with hotel, airline, and travel agency on the number of confirmed reservations each has received
2 months	❑ Finalize contracts with ground transportation and tour operators

(*continued*)

Figure 1.1 (*continued*)

Time Before Meeting	Meeting Planning Activity
2 months (*continued*)	❑ Reconfirm all speakers/presentors and send travel reimbursement forms ❑ Design and send final program to the printer ❑ Buy or order presentor/VIP gifts/awards/plaques ❑ Give ground operators VIP transportation arrangements ❑ Establish registration personnel requirements ❑ Schedule and hire staff; set staff pay ❑ Make staff travel arrangements ❑ Review registration numbers and adjust all contracts
1 month	❑ Inventory, check, and recheck all printed materials ❑ Choose shipping arrangements for meeting materials and begin to ship them if arrangements have been made with hotel ❑ Continue communications with hotel ❑ Send presentors their transportation tickets ❑ Contact and contract with florist ❑ Complete and print attendee and exhibitor lists ❑ Reconfirm all contractors ❑ Review all registrations ❑ Send out news releases
1 week	❑ Give ground transportation final schedule ❑ Pack office supplies ❑ Train staff ❑ Get cash and change from bank ❑ Pack checkbook ❑ Confirm arrival of meeting materials ❑ Give hotel information for meeting signs
1 day	❑ Meet with convention services manager and all hotel staff ❑ Reconfirm food and beverage numbers ❑ Inventory materials ❑ Train on-site staff ❑ Open registration desk ❑ Place signs and floral arrangements ❑ Meet with VIP escorts ❑ Organize hospitality rooms ❑ Get VIP room keys and distribute gifts

Figure 1.1 (continued)

Time Before Meeting	Meeting Planning Activity
1 day (*continued*)	❑ Open safety deposit box ❑ Rehearse as necessary
Before each session	❑ Check room setup against function sheet ❑ Try out microphones and audiovisual equipment ❑ Place handouts, namecards, evaluations, other materials
After the meeting	❑ Approve and sign property bills ❑ Give out gratuities ❑ Ship materials ❑ Pay bills ❑ Reimburse travel ❑ Enter walk-ins in registration database ❑ Complete income/expense statement ❑ Compile attendee evaluations ❑ Write detailed planner evaluation

Figure 1.1 (*continued*)

In the course of planning a meeting, a planner will need to approach many strangers. A touch of humor and a bit of compassion are also essential.

Meeting planners must also be organizers, able to perform tasks step by step. People who keep lists make good meeting planners. Being attentive to details is essential, but meeting planners must be able to see the big picture too.

Finally, meeting planners must thrive on challenge and have a passion for excellence. Mediocrity is not tolerated in the meeting business. And it goes without saying that nerves of steel and high energy are basic requirements. Meeting planners must appear calm in the midst of chaos and implement immediate solutions to problems. They must also have the vitality and endurance for 12-hour workdays.

There's another side of meeting planning that is not revealed in the job announcement or the personal advertisement, however—perpetual tension, waking at night to write notes to yourself, a constant feeling that you've forgotten something, maintaining outward calm when your blood pressure is 190/110, smiling, smiling, and scrutinizing your notebook for last-minute double-checks. There are lonely nights in strange hotels and the pressure of playing hardball when negotiating contracts. But if you like a challenge, enjoy people, and crave variety, then you can be a successful meeting planner. Meeting planning suits those who thrive on recognition, respect, and visibility.

Why Are Meetings Important?

Meetings have a huge economic impact. Almost one million meetings are held in the United States each year with over 90 million participants and over $43.7 billion dollars spent (see Figure 1.2). On the average, an attendee at a three-day meeting spends $719 on site. Not only do these expenditures strengthen local economies, but in the aggregate they also provide employment. If you spend $100 in a hotel, a portion of that goes to pay the desk clerk. That clerk buys groceries, and the grocer pays rent. The grocer's landlord buys a pair of slacks. Thus, your $100 is multiplied and used again and again. Figure 1.3 shows which sectors of the economy benefit from meeting expenditures.

Most cities have Convention and Visitors Bureaus (CVBs) that encourage organizations to meet in their towns. Why? The meeting participant is looked upon by CVBs as a desirable visitor. Many people attending meetings are on expense accounts and thus spend more than the average tourist.

Convention and visitors bureaus are nonprofit membership organizations made up of many travel-related companies—transportation, accommodations, food services, and attractions. These companies pay dues that are channeled into providing advertising, sales promotion materials, and visitor services. CVBs may exist only for a single city, or they may market

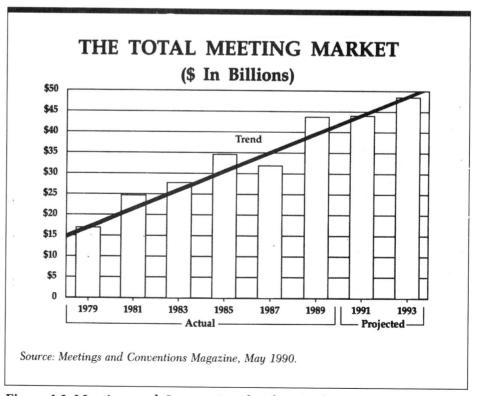

Figure 1.2 Meetings and Conventions by the Numbers

Estimated 1989 Meeting Expenditures ($ Billions)			
	Corporate Expenditures	Association Meetings	Major Conventions	Total Meetings
Hotel, Food, & Associated (57%)	$7.9	$8.4	$8.6	$24.9
Air Transportation (24%)	$3.4	$3.5	$3.6	$10.5
Speakers, Entertainment, & A/V Services (8%)	$1.1	$1.2	$1.2	$3.5
Ground Transportation (5%)	$0.7	$0.8	$0.7	$2.2
Other (6%)	$0.8	$0.9	$0.9	$2.6
Total	$13.9	$14.8	$15.0	$43.7

Source: *Meetings and Conventions Magazine, May 1990.*

Figure 1.3 Group Meetings Expenditures

the desirability of an entire county or region as a meeting site. Often there is city or county funding for the CVB.

Convention and visitors bureaus also provide the first contact when seeking a site for a meeting. They can let the meeting planner know about properties that would be appropriate for the meeting. CVBs may often be able to act as housing bureaus for multiple property meetings, and may also be able to provide materials, such as nametags or brochure shells, at cost. Certainly they can offer tourist information folders.

State tourism offices can provide assistance in negotiating with large, prestigious organizations to hold their meetings at some location in the state. At the national level, the U.S. Travel and Tourism Administration (USTTA) works to lure international meetings to this country. It also asks that associations invite their foreign counterparts to attend meetings in the United States.

Destination marketing organizations (DMOs) try to entice meetings to their areas because of the economic benefits.

Meetings are also significant educational and motivational tools. They provide professional training, which improves national productivity. They are effectively used to motivate groups toward goals. Meetings also provide the opportunity for communication. Williams Matthews said, "A full mind must have talk, or it will grow dyspeptic."

CHAPTER ACTIVITIES

1. Evaluate your skills. Could you fulfill the requirements of the job advertisement at the beginning of this chapter?

2. Evaluate your personality. Could you fulfill the requirements of the personal ad in this chapter?

3. Write a letter to a prospective employer who is seeking a meeting planner, explaining how you qualify for the position.

4. Rate each task of the Meeting Planning Task Checklist on a 1 to 5 scale as to your confidence in performing it competently. A "5" means that you feel entirely confident. A "1" means that you do not feel that you have developed the skills required for the task.

2

Who Meets?

Upon completion of this chapter,
you will be able to:

1. Classify the various types of associations and businesses

2. Explain in general terms the characteristics of association members

3. Produce a participant profile

W ho holds meetings? Who goes to meetings? Two friends can meet to discuss their upcoming vacation, or 20,000 people can meet to nominate a presidential candidate.

Primarily, meetings are held for and by organizations—people united for a common purpose. Usually the organization's members get together to share their feelings, thoughts, aims, goals, and information. Why do they meet? Usually, for business or for fun.

Identifying the type of organization and its geographical scope is the first step for meeting planning. Many decisions and details of organizing a meeting will be based on these facts.

Organizations

Organizations fall into two general categories: associations and businesses. *Associations* are organizations of people who are affiliated by reason of professional or personal interests. *Businesses* are corporations or companies. The people who work for them make up the organization. Associations and corporations have somewhat different meeting needs, which will be pointed out.

Associations

Associations can be classified by their purposes and aims. Over 19,000 associations are listed in the *Encyclopedia of Associations.* The majority of them meet annually.

❑ **Professional associations** are composed of people with a common occupation or career. Professional associations may have tens of thousands of members or fewer than 100 members, depending on the numbers of people in the field. The term *profession* usually denotes advanced study and specialized training. Professional associations exist for people in careers such as medicine, engineering, education, and law; the list could go on and on. The American Medical Association, National Education Association, and American Dental Association are examples of professional associations.

Professional associations generally are formed to share knowledge and often have stringent standards for membership. They may also regulate a particular profession by setting performance standards and formulating codes of professional ethics. Some associations exist primarily as accrediting bodies. The Association of Independent Colleges and Schools is an example. It grants accreditation to schools, and its members meet annually.

Professional associations may have local, state, national, and even international levels. They may also have chapters, or regional subgroups that meet either regularly or as needed. They might meet at a member's home or at orchestrated luncheons or dinners.

National meetings of professional associations are usually held annually. These meetings emphasize training, education, and updating skills. Subspecialties might hold their own meetings under the umbrella of the larger organization. For example, ear, nose, and throat specialists might meet apart from the annual American Medical Association meeting.

❑ **Trade associations,** like professional associations, are groups of people with similar jobs or careers. Members might be farmers, electricians, or plumbers. Trade associations often set performance standards in their particular field and promote public awareness of their occupations. Labor unions, such as the AFL-CIO, fall under the category of trade associations.

Trade associations hold meetings to exchange information and conduct association business. Meetings are usually held annually, and local chapters participate actively. There is a National Chimney Sweep Guild (*guild* is an old term for trade association) and a Licensed Beverage Association, along with many other occupational associations.

❑ **Fraternal and social organizations** often act as service organizations, donating time and money to charities. These groups are usually made up of people who have friendship as their common bond.

The Elks, Lions, Masons, Civitans, and Rotary Club are fraternal organizations. They usually hold large conventions that often feature parades and elaborate social functions. Members from all over the world attend their annual meetings.

Greek fraternities and sororities, based on college campuses, are another branch of the fraternal/social organization network. Brotherhood, sisterhood, and leadership training are their goals. Phi Beta Kappa is the oldest collegiate fraternity.

❑ **Common interest groups** are organized around a huge variety of hobbies and professional pursuits. Growing pansies, collecting model trains, and reading science fiction all attract enough people to form organizations and hold meetings.

Common interest groups emphasize sharing knowledge. Often the groups meet to sell, swap, or trade some object, such as rare coins or stamps. Their meetings might be held on the local, national, or international level. Usually a trade show is an integral part of the common interest group's meeting.

❑ **Political groups** attract people from various backgrounds with similar political party affiliations or legislative goals. The Republican and Democratic parties hold meetings on the local level, and both parties hold national presidential conventions to nominate electoral candidates.

An example of a political group formed to promote certain legislative reforms is Mothers Against Drunk Drivers (MADD). Members meet to form legislative policy and to educate and promote awareness of their particular cause.

❏ **Religious and ethnic organization** members are bound by common theological or sociological backgrounds or interests. These groups seek to promote awareness of their beliefs and background. Religious groups meet to set policy, standards, and doctrine for followers.

The National Association for the Advancement of Colored People is an example of an ethnic organization that is also politically oriented. It promotes awareness, monitors legislation, and lobbies. Ethnic groups also meet for pleasure, often promoting the retention of customs and traditions. The Robert Burns Society is an example. It promotes the Scottish culture.

❏ **Charitable organizations** such as the National Heart Association and the Society for the Prevention of Cruelty to Animals exist for a myriad of causes. Their primary goals are to improve the public's understanding of various diseases, disabilities, and social problems and to raise money for research and assistance.

Charitable organizations have strong local chapters and national and international networks. Their meetings center on the association's business matters and might also feature research presentations, particularly if the association is concerned with a health issue.

Businesses

Businesses large and small throughout the world hold meetings. They might be meetings of top management or of front-line production personnel. There might be meetings of stockholders to make major corporate decisions or of a company sales force to generate excitement about new products.

Businesses hold meetings for many reasons. Among them are sales incentive and training. Corporate meetings to introduce a product can be huge and elaborate, with many planning demands; many business meetings, however, are small and relatively simple to organize.

Business and industry can be divided into four broad categories: 1) manufacturing, 2) distributing, 3) providing service, and 4) government. Many businesses involve more than one of these activities. Some businesses are conglomerates, owning companies from each category.

Some businesses might not fall into the classifications indicated here. When assessing the category in which a business is included, look at its end product. For example, McDonald's ultimate activity is serving food. Thus, it is a service business, even though it distributes and also manufactures items.

Many of the organizations described also sponsor trade shows or exhibits. Chapter 3 discusses these special kinds of meetings.

❏ **Manufacturers** produce, concoct, or fabricate items from raw materials. Almost everything that you can see or touch, from your automobile to a paper clip, has been manufactured. Obviously, there are millions of manufacturing businesses, many with multiple plants or factories. Farming is also a type of manufacturing business.

Manufacturing businesses have production, supervisory, and management personnel. Many manufacturers are also involved in two other types of business activities: distribution and service. A manufacturing business can be a small two-person tailor shop producing custom-made suits or the giant Ford Motor Company.

Manufacturers hold meetings to train both line staff and management. Production quotas or profit margins might be the subject of a management meeting. Trade shows are staged by manufacturers to display their goods.

❑ **Distributors** dispense, deliver, and supply. This classification also includes sales, a large component of our economy. Moving goods from the manufacturer to the buyer includes packaging, transportation, warehousing, and ultimately selling (both wholesale and retail). As mentioned, both distribution and service activities might be a part of a manufacturing business.

A distributor can be two-person handicraft shops where the owners distribute (sell) pottery and baskets or the vast K Mart corporation, which sells a variety of goods to the public. The size of the company and the number of employees vary widely among distributors.

Distributors might hold training meetings for representatives or incentive meetings that award top sales representation. Internal communications or procedures might be the subject of a distributor's meeting.

❑ **Service businesses** benefit, maintain, and help you and your property. While manufacturers and distributors deal with products, service businesses perform action or advise and manage. Hotels, restaurants, banks, brokerage houses, insurance companies, laundries—all are service businesses.

The service industry can be divided into areas such as hospitality, finance, communications, and personal services. Hospitality would include lodging and restaurant businesses. Amusements and attractions would also be classified as hospitality services.

Finance industries are banking, insurance, and stock brokerage firms. Communications includes the media, newspapers, magazines, radio, television, and advertising companies. Personal services encompasses repair, real estate, and health care companies, among others.

Utility companies, both public and private, are another kind of service industry. These companies may also manufacture or refine a product and distribute it to the public. Their final objective, however, is providing a service.

The size of service businesses can vary from a shoe repair business with only two employees to nationwide stock, real estate, and investment companies with tens of thousands of employees. Service companies hold employee meetings and also send participants to appropriate association meetings. Customer relations and information processing are often meeting topics.

❑ **Government** represents another major business sector, for a business need not be a commercial enterprise. Government agencies at all levels (city, county, state, and federal) hold meetings of all types. The armed forces also make up a large part of government.

The meeting needs of the government/military complex are somewhat different from those of other organizations. The per diem allowed for government travel must be kept in mind when planning a government-related meeting. Government agencies usually call meetings to educate, change operating procedures, or plan.

❏ **Seminar businesses** exist solely to stage public meetings and sell a product. Often the products being sold are more seminars, tapes, or books. For-profit seminars cover such topics as personal development or finance. These businesses hold public seminars in major cities.

Geographical Scope

Most organizations are established along local, regional, statewide, national, or international lines. Associations and businesses that have more than one office, factory, or retail outlet may have geographical divisions.

If an organization has a broad geographical scope, its membership balloons. Defining an organization's scope helps determine the number of people who might attend its meetings. More members equals more meeting participants. A national meeting usually is going to be larger than a state meeting.

Organizations often pyramid geographically. The county organization meets, and then a county representative or representatives are selected to be sent to the state meeting. The state organization then chooses a representative to go to the national meeting. Likewise, a national convention might select a representative to attend an international meeting.

In all phases of meeting planning, the geographical makeup of the audience at a meeting is a vital consideration. Some meetings cross geographical boundaries. A meeting held in Toronto, for example, may draw organizational members from Canada even though the meeting is primarily for American members. Many U.S. organizations become international organizations by virtue of a few Canadian or Mexican members. Likewise, Canadian or Mexican organizations may be considered international because their membership includes American citizens.

The Participant Profile

A quick look at the profile of a typical meeting participant gives the meeting planner insight concerning meetings. It gives ideas about where to hold the meeting and how to schedule and pace it. The profile also gives clues as to how formal the meeting program should be and the level of luxury desired.

A participant profile reveals if language barriers must be overcome or if facilities for disabled participants should be provided.

The components of the participant profile include age, sex, occupation, average income, hometown, whether the participant will be accompanied by anyone, and who pays.

❑ **Age.** Many meetings include participants of all ages, although many organizations restrict their membership to certain age groups. The type of organization can make the age of meeting attendees readily apparent. One can assume that a meeting of medical doctors would involve people over the age of 25 because most people under that age do not have medical degrees, whereas the Future Business Leaders of America is a high school organization with a 15- to 18-year-old membership.

If the average age of attendees is 18 to 25, then the meeting takes on a different flavor from that of a meeting of senior citizens. For example, a college fraternity convention is quite different from other meetings. A high level of activity, a faster pace, and informality would be expected. A meeting for members of a senior citizens' group will take on a different tone. The pace might be slower, the atmosphere more formal, and more luxury might be provided.

❑ **Sex.** Some meetings have only male or only female attendees. For example, a cosmetic company convention will be composed primarily of women. On the other hand, men dominate the heavy equipment sales force. Many meetings have both sexes equally represented. In general, free-time activities, entertainment, and menu should meet the need of both genders.

❑ **Occupation.** A person's job can indicate his or her interests, knowledge, likes, and dislikes and so can be a clue to meeting requirements. Many meetings involve only people of the same occupation. A meeting of college professors, for example, has a different level of formality, luxury, and pacing than a meeting of pinball machine arcade owners.

Planning a meeting for people who do the same thing for a living or who enjoy the same hobby is somewhat easier than trying to please people with a variety of professions, trades, or leisure-time pursuits. As a rule, the interests of the members of an occupational group lie in the same area and their social and economic backgrounds are similar.

Certainly corporate meetings involve people who work for the same company, but not necessarily in the same occupation. There might be accountants, support staff, and sales representatives who all work for the same company and attend the same meeting. The program might be planned to meet the needs of the different occupational groups represented by having breakout sessions directed toward the different fields.

❑ **Average income.** Participants in the same occupation tend to have incomes within the same realm. The meeting planner must consider the average income of attendees in making location and property decisions. Income estimates help the meeting planner plan free-time activities and suggest the level of luxury expected at the meeting. Registration fees are set with the participants' average income in mind.

Members of common interest groups have disparate income levels. The average income of members of the Antique Maserati Owners Association is most likely quite high, but dollhouse collectors represent a variety of income backgrounds, and it would be difficult to pinpoint their average salaries.

❑ **Hometown.** Are the attendees primarily from large urban areas or are they from small towns and farms? This information helps the planner to choose a meeting location and free-time activities.

Usually people from small towns, which often have limited entertainment and recreational facilities, relish visiting a big city with a variety of amusements. Those from urban areas often appreciate the quiet and calmness of a resort area, preferring a program with more leisurely timing with relaxation intervals built in.

How far participants have to travel from their hometowns to a meeting site is another factor that affects pricing and other planning decisions.

❑ **Accompanying spouses and companions.** More and more businesses and associations include their employees' and members' spouses in the meeting invitation. For incentive meetings that award top performers, over 88 percent invite spouses to attend the meeting or join in on the prize trip. On the other hand, certain meetings are open to only a few people or have such limited interest that spouses are not included. Even though not specifically invited, a spouse might accompany a participant to the meeting site and attend related social events.

The participant profile should indicate what percentage of the attendees will bring their spouses or companions. This information will govern rooming needs, meal estimates, and free-time management. Companion programs have become an integral part of meeting planning. Many cities have organizations that arrange activities for spouses during the meeting hours.

The participant profile should also indicate whether participants are willing to share rooms. Some are unwilling to do this, while others are happy to cut expenses.

❑ **Who pays?** Usually business meetings are paid for by the company that sponsors the meeting, and most of the participants will be using expense accounts. Association meetings have a mixture of self-pay and company-pay attendees. Often people belong to an organization because it is beneficial to their career, and their companies pick up their meeting costs because of the advantages the companies will eventually receive when the attendees return to the workplace and share the knowledge gained.

When common interest groups meet, the participants are usually self-pay, as they are willing to incur the cost of the meeting to develop their hobby. If the majority of attendees are self-pay, the meeting planner keeps economy in mind, unless it is a group such as the Antique Maserati Owners

Association, whose members are most likely to have abundant funds to spend at a meeting.

Consider the following participant profiles. See if you would agree with the conclusions drawn about what kind of meetings would be most suitable for these organizations.

Antique Maserati Owners Association

Age	45–70
Sex	Male (90%)
Occupation	Professionals (medical doctors/attorneys)
Average income	$100,000+
Hometown	Mixed location and size
Accompanied by spouse?	50%
Who pays?	Self

From the name of the association, we can see that this group will meet primarily for pleasure. There will be a certain amount of trading information and possibly a small exhibit of used parts. It is a group of upper-income attendees. Economy is not a big consideration. Some activities should be provided for spouses. A certain degree of luxury will be expected, but the meeting will be fairly informal. Free time for mingling should be scheduled.

Teachers of Typing Association

Age	22–55
Sex	Female
Occupation	High school teachers
Average income	$28,000
Hometown	Mixed urban and rural
Accompanied by spouse?	10%
Who pays?	80% School district/20% Self

Obviously, the cost of this meeting should be held to a minimum. If it is too expensive, school systems will not pay, and those who are interested enough in the subject to pay their own way will not be able to attend. A medium degree of luxury will be expected, and good taste will be demanded. To achieve educational objectives, a fast-paced, well organized meeting will be needed. Little free time will be expected.

Mutual Insurance Northeast Regional Sales Force

Age	28–50
Sex	Male (95%)
Occupation	Sales
Average income	$36,000
Hometown	10,000–200,000/small urban
Accompanied by spouse?	55%
Who pays?	Company (on expense account)

The purpose of this meeting is most likely to either reward the sales representatives or incite them to sell more. The meeting planner has to work with management as far as costs, since the company pays all expenses. Activities that include spouses should be planned.

To summarize, meeting planning means knowing the organization and knowing the people who will attend the meeting. All meeting planning decisions will be based on the information that is determined from the participant profile.

CHAPTER ACTIVITIES

1.   Identify three of each of the following types of associations in your area:

Professional

Trade

Fraternal

Social

Common interest

Religious

Ethnic

Charitable

2.   Interview a person in each of four business categories. Find out how many meetings per year are held for each kind of company. Find out if

these are local, regional, statewide, national, or international meetings. Obtain a profile of those that attend the meetings.

Manufacturers

Distributors

Service Businesses

Government

3

Purposes and Types of Meetings

**Upon completion of this chapter,
you will be able to:**

1. Understand the reasons for holding meetings
2. Know the names used for meetings
3. Understand the basics of trade shows and exhibitions

W hy meet? Is it because of tradition? "We just get together every year." Is a meeting the quickest way to tell something, solve a problem, exchange ideas, or socialize? What defines a meeting? A common definition of a *meeting* is a planned event with two or more people with a common objective.

The goals and objectives of a meeting must be clearly established. An organization that has immediate objectives, goals, and aims may believe that holding a meeting is the most efficient way to achieve them. For example, if business is going to implement new accounting codes and it is likely that long-time employees will be resistant to the change, a company-wide meeting may be beneficial. The meeting is called for a reason and the design and planning of it takes on purpose and becomes less complicated. If the goals are vague, oversimplistic, and unimportant, perhaps there is no need for a meeting. Even mandatory meetings, such as those for shareholders, must have objectives, which may be as simple as approving the budget or electing new officers.

The objectives and agendas for corporation meetings are usually scrutinized closely by management. Of course, time equals money, and meetings take both time and money, so the objectives must be worthwhile. Not only are there expenses for registration, transportation, and accommodations, but the cost of time away from work must also be added. Ideally, a meeting should be considered an investment in an employee's or association member's knowledge or personal development.

For many meetings, prospective participants have a choice of attending. The meeting's value must be apparent before attendees will come. So, all communication with prospective attendees should clearly explain the objectives, goals, and aims of the meeting. The way in which the meeting will achieve, or satisfy, these objectives should be obvious.

Reasons for Meeting

Meetings are generally held for at least one of the following reasons:

1. To educate and train
2. To carry on the internal business and operations of an organization
3. To motivate
4. To reward and celebrate
5. To produce revenue

Educating and Training

The majority of meetings are held to educate, to train, or to share information. Association members might need to learn of upcoming legislation, or employees might need to learn of changes in company policy. The activities planned at educational meetings include teaching, updating or reviewing skills, explaining new ideas and techniques, and showing resources. Exchanging information while networking or socializing with peers is also integral to education and training.

Teaching a new technique or exploring a new idea is usually done by an expert in a traditional lecture setting or by panels at which facilitators lead audience discussion. Updating a new procedure or reviewing information can also be done in lectures and audience participation sessions. At meetings of professional associations, doctoral candidates may present research papers on new findings in a particular field.

Sometimes Continuing Education Units (CEUs) can be earned by the participants at an educational meeting. Many professional associations require their members to attain a certain number of hours of continuing education each year as a condition for continued licensure or good standing in the profession.

At some meetings, products might be introduced and demonstrated. A new car might be presented with much hoopla and the changes and advantages over last year's model explained to the sales force. There can be a fine line between educating sales representatives about a product and motivating them to sell it.

Trade shows lend themselves to group training. Exhibits can be mounted that show resources and products. For example, textbooks and other instructional aids are displayed at trade shows for educators. Similarly, the latest medical and surgical equipment and pharmaceutical supplies are arrayed for those who attend medical conventions.

Educating the public can also be a meeting objective that is accomplished by soliciting press coverage. When a meeting on asbestos disease is held and extensively publicized, for example, it increases public awareness.

For some taxpayers, educational meeting expenses can be used as a write-off on taxes. The costs of registration and travel can often be deducted from gross income. Chapter 4 summarizes the Internal Revenue Code's regulations in this regard.

Handling Organizational Business

"All in favor, please say aye." Handling organizational operations and business is another reason for holding a meeting. Although the routine business of most organizations is carried out without fanfare by its executive officers and staff, there are occasions when organization-wide or division-wide meetings are warranted.

For example, new officers might need to be elected. Or there may be a reason for planning and designing new strategies for the organization. Public companies are required by law to hold an annual meeting for all shareholders, who must be notified of the meeting. Meeting planners wring their hands trying to invent some way to increase interest in such "command" attendance events. The annual report, the year's financial figures, or a year's review are usually presented. Board members of an organization might need to meet several times a year to discuss and make significant operational decisions.

Motivating Members and Employees

"This model is superior to anything on the market. Our aim is to put 25,000 of these on the road by March!" Associations and businesses meet to inspire enthusiasm and to rally their membership and employees to carry out certain objectives. The goal might be to sell more products, foster favorable legislation, or encourage self-improvement. Promoting teamwork is one kind of motivational goal.

In introducing a new product, besides wanting to educate the meeting attendees concerning product improvements, management wants to stimulate its sales force to sell, sign contracts, and be enthusiastic about the product. Incentive meetings, which are discussed below, are akin to motivational meetings.

Providing Rewards and Celebrating Achievements

If you had sold 25 automobiles the last month, you might have won a free trip to this year's Superbowl. Buying 25,000 pounds of fertilizer might have entitled you and your family to a free trip to Cancun. Incentive, or award, travel is big business.

Incentive meetings are rewards for superior achievement. They may involve trips to exotic locations or elaborate banquets with entertainment. Incentive meetings are held for those who have been highly motivated and have successfully achieved some predetermined goal. Some type of formal business meeting is usually involved, but it is usually short.

Sometimes the people who win incentive trips can choose when they want to take advantage of the trip. Otherwise, group travel is scheduled for a specific date. In this case, everyone who is entitled to the bonus trip goes away together. Incentive trips are usually planned to be first class throughout. Four-star properties are reserved, and all costs—meals, entertainment, greens fees, court fees, and so on—are covered. Some incentive trips even give attendees spending money. Some companies, called *incentive houses* or *fulfillment firms*, plan incentive meetings and organize these kinds of prize trips.

An incentive meeting might simply be planned around a sumptuous food and beverage presentation. This is planned as a brunch, coffee, tea, cocktail party, wine-tasting party, luncheon, banquet, or reception, perhaps in someone's honor. A performing artist or group could be featured. Participation events, such as a dance or a sporting event, could also be the feature of a meeting. People also meet to celebrate. Examples of celebrations are political victory parties and weddings.

Producing Revenue

Finally, a meeting might be held strictly as a fund-raising event. For example, dinners are held to raise funds for candidates running for public office. Or for $1,000, one might be invited to meet a member of royalty; the resulting profits are then donated to a charitable organization. Auctions and casino nights are also examples of revenue-producing meetings.

Trade shows are usually income-producing events. Entrance and exhibitors' fees can benefit either a private organization or a nonprofit charity.

Types of Meetings

"To join, be united, encounter, come face to face, come together, come into contact or connection with" is one definition of the term *meeting*. The term is sufficiently generic to cover any type of gathering. Yet there are many kinds of meetings, and different names are given to them depending on such factors as their size and objectives. For our purposes, the 10 most common types are listed below. Trade shows, exhibitions, and mini–trade shows are additional types of meetings.

Keep in mind that one can call a meeting by any name desired. The name of a meeting is up to the meeting organizers.

❑ **Convention.** This term usually is used to describe meetings that are national in scope. In many cases, convention goers are chosen to attend as representatives of their local organizational chapters. Most conventions are quite large. The Democratic and Republican party conventions are prime examples, although a statewide meeting of public health nurses can also be called a convention.

❑ **Congress.** The term *congress* often denotes national or international participation. The political implications are obvious, but a congress can be held by any group on any subject. To some, the term indicates that many delegates, each representing a local chapter or geographical area, will attend.

❑ **Conference.** *Confer* means to bring together. Two people can confer, but conferences often count large numbers of participants. Attendees at a conference have like careers or interests. A conference could be made up solely of chemical engineers or a conference on chemical genetic engineering might involve chemists, engineers, doctors, researchers. *Conference* is one of the most commonly used terms for *meeting*.

❑ **Council.** The term *council* means to call or summon together. It can be used as the name of a group or as the name of a meeting. For example, one can act as a consultant to the Tourism Council, and one can also attend the Tourism Council.

❑ **Seminar.** Many college students attend seminars—small, highly focused classes that promote the exchange of ideas on a particular topic. Seminars can last one hour or several days. They might be offered as part of a larger meeting. The term suggests that people are there to draw information, not to give information.

A seminar may be open to the public. For example, a seminar on "How to Invest in Real Estate" may be advertised in many cities. People attending ostensibly have nothing in common except the desire to learn about investing in real estate.

❑ **Forum.** A forum is very similar to a seminar. One definition for *forum* is a public program with panel discussions and audience participation. To some, a forum suggests an open, informal meeting, such as a town forum on zoning regulations.

❑ **Symposium.** A particular topic is discussed by several specialists at a *symposium*. It has a rather formal implication and is used primarily when scientific topics are discussed. An example would be a symposium on combating acquired immuno-deficiency syndrome (AIDS). The term is also often used for political meetings. A symposium on preventing desecration of the Central American rain forest might involve the international environmental community.

❑ **Retreat.** Retreats are often held for intensive problem solving, introspection, and study. Customarily, only a few people attend retreats. A retreat may include a brainstorming session at which a moderator or facilitator leads attendees in seeking new ideas. For example, the board of a Chamber of Commerce might go on a retreat to develop the next year's strategies for attracting new industry to a region.

❑ **Workshop.** A *workshop* is a short educational program where small groups talk over specific problems. Workshops may be small sessions held during conferences or conventions or entire meetings unto themselves. A workshop may also mean a short meeting—one that lasts only two or three hours. One can attend a workshop on historic preservation, knitting, or learning WordPerfect 5.0. The variety is limitless.

❑ **Clinic.** Due to its medical usage, the term *clinic* implies that aid, help, or diagnosis of problems will be offered. But the range of problems is quite broad. There can be clinics in telephone techniques or stenciling.

❑ **Lecture.** A very simple meeting can involve an expert lecturing about a specific topic to an audience. Examples would be a university lecture on nineteenth-century political parties or a garden club holding a lecture on Ikebana.

Exhibitions and Trade Shows

Exhibitions and trade shows are big business in North America. More than 9,000 are held each year. They are staged to describe services or display wares or products. They can be significant sources of revenue for their sponsoring organizations.

The term *exhibition* generally is used to describe a show that is held in conjunction with another meeting, such as a convention. *Trade show* is the term used for a show that is held for its own sake, that is, the trade show itself is the event. *Exposition* is a term used for both. These terms are often used interchangeably, but for purposes of this book, exhibitions mean shows that are held along with other events or meetings, and trade shows mean standalone events.

Staging large exhibitions and trade shows uses meeting planning concepts, but it has its own professional principles and requirements. This book cannot begin to cover the details of planning and executing exhibitions. A great deal of technical knowledge is needed about such subjects as engineering and labor negotiation. There are exhibit service companies that provide such expertise. They contract for transportation, audiovisual equipment, storage, insurance, freight, setup, break down, models, and photographers.

Exhibitions

An exhibition has a built-in audience, since it is held in conjunction with a meeting. Because most meetings attract people with like interests or occupations, an exhibition will naturally be made up of vendors whose wares or services would be appealing to the meeting attendees.

Generally, an allotted amount of space is bought by an exhibitor. Displays may range from small, six-foot tabletop exhibits to huge booths featuring technically sophisticated audiovisual presentations. Many organizations find that staging an exhibition at a meeting can offset a great deal of the costs of the meeting. When this is the case, the exhibition becomes a major consideration in all of the meeting planning.

A small exhibition might simply consist of tabletop exhibits of products or resources that are displayed at a luncheon or cocktail party scheduled as part of a larger meeting. For example, a small exhibition at a firefighters' luncheon might include a pictorial display of life-saving techniques and exhibit a new disposable respiration device. Larger exhibitions are held in the exhibition halls or ballrooms of the hotels where meetings are held. If a convention is spread out among several facilities, a civic center or convention might be rented for the exhibition. If an outside hall is used, usually some meeting session or meal will be planned there that draws attendees to the exhibition and gives vendors ample exposure.

An exhibition might run throughout an entire meeting, or its hours might be restricted. Meeting planners have to decide how an exhibition will be scheduled. They must balance giving attendees plenty of time to view the exhibition against not having them miss important sessions. Naturally, when space is expensive, exhibitors expect that more time will be allotted for viewing.

Trade Shows

An example of a trade show is a travel industry show. Here, various travel suppliers, airlines, hotel chains, travel agencies, and tour operators all exhibit their products and services. Sporting goods, home improvement products, and antiques are also popular for trade shows. Trade shows are usually held in convention halls or civic centers and are open to the public.

Other trade shows restrict admission. For example, furniture marts, featuring furniture manufacturers, might allow only furniture retailers and interior decorators to enter. Clothing designers and manufacturers might restrict admission to retail store buyers. Sometimes a trade show may restrict its audience for a few days and then open the show to the public.

Trade shows might run for a single day or be open for a week. Shows featuring products are usually held on week days during normal business hours. Shows that are open to the public tend to operate from the late afternoon until 9 or 10 P.M. They are usually heavily advertised. A grand opening might be held or a press or VIP reception planned. Often name entertainment is featured at a public trade show to draw a large audience. Gimmicks used to attract the public include passing out giveaways such as balloons or providing roaming entertainment such as clowns.

Obviously, staging trade shows is a profit-making business. Because exhibitors pay for the privilege of showing their goods or services, they expect excellent publicity and show management. Managing trade shows requires people who are good with details and organization. Design, engineering, and negotiating skills are also needed.

Mini–Trade Shows

These are sometimes called *room shows, fairs,* or *mini-marts.* One or more vendors of similar products rent rooms at a hotel where they set up their displays. Either the public or a specific audience is invited to view the exhibits. Naturally, there is a limit to what can be exhibited in room shows. Imported carpets are a popular item, as are fashions, furs, and art.

CHAPTER ACTIVITIES

Ask some meeting properties (e.g., hotels, exhibit halls, convention centers) to let you research the names of meetings that they are hosting. Ask the Convention and Visitors Bureau for an upcoming meeting list. From this information answer the following questions.

1. What are the most popular names for meetings?

2. List the numbers of anticipated attendance for each named meeting (e.g., Mutual of America Sales Representatives, 65; West Central Pork Producers Convention, 500)

3. Is there a correlation between the name of a meeting and the number of attendees?

4

Planning the Meeting Program

Upon completion of this chapter,
you will be able to:

1. Define meeting program components and explain how
   they meet overall meeting objectives

2. Plan a meeting's pace and tempo

3. Make arrangements for speakers

4. Draft a meeting program

A t this point in the meeting planning process, you have the following information: 1) which organization will sponsor the meeting; 2) why the meeting will be held; 3) what type of meeting will be held; and 4) how many participants are expected to attend the meeting.

The reason for holding the meeting and its objectives, goals, and purpose must be re-examined and dissected. Now you must draft a skeleton or "dummy" program. This draft program shows the approximate timing of the meeting sessions, plans for food and beverage service, free-time activities, and entertainment needs. You can also estimate the approximate size and number of meeting rooms that will be needed. Each program component has a cost, which can be estimated on the dummy program so that a budget can be established.

The dummy program should include your best guess about what program components will help achieve the meeting objective. For example, introducing a new product, having the CEO deliver an address, reviewing the budget, presenting the coming year's advertising campaign, and holding a panel on successful sales techniques are all program components that can help achieve precise objectives.

The chart below shows how you might relate the meeting's objectives and methods in drafting the dummy program. Estimate the time needed for each activity. For example, a reception usually lasts one hour and an awards banquet might last three hours.

Objective	Method	Estimated Time
Excite sales force	See new ads	1 hour
Reward top performers	Reception Banquet	2 hours
Sales training	Guest Speaker Panel	1½ hours
Team building	Challenge course Cookout	Half day

The dummy program is not intended at this time to be specific about titles of presentations or to name speakers. The point is to outline the general program needs, allot time slots, and state presentation methods.

The Size of the Meeting

The number of people expected to attend a meeting is probably the key to such meeting planning decisions as the type of meeting to be held and what to call the meeting. Certainly a meeting of only six regional sales representatives would not be called a convention. Except in rare cases, an exhibition would not be held for ten people.

As discussed in Chapter 2, the geographical scope of a group gives some indication of how many participants to expect. A state meeting will probably be smaller than a national meeting. Yet meeting history is the best indicator of how many people to expect at a meeting. Some organizations might expect 95 percent of their members to attend a meeting. Others expect only a one percent attendance of the total membership. Comparing attendance figures at similar meetings can provide valuable information.

The program and its level of interest will also affect attendance numbers. A program with dynamic subjects and speakers or interesting activities draws larger crowds.

The location of the meeting will affect attendance. A location accessible to the greatest number of members increases attendance. More people will attend a meeting in New Orleans, which has a lot to offer tourists, than in a small midwestern town. The ease with which people can get to the meeting (for example, a nonstop flight between metropolitan airports versus flights interrupted with layovers) is also a factor. Site selection is the focus of Chapter 5.

During a recession, businesses and government slash their travel budgets. Attendance figures can take a downturn. If a similar organization announces a meeting that competes for the same audience, attendance figures may be lower than expected.

Considering all of these factors, the meeting planner and the organization's management must determine a rough estimate of the number of attendees to expect at a given meeting. Almost all decisions in the planning exercise will depend on this estimated number.

The Length of the Meeting

How long does it take to achieve the objectives of a meeting? The average duration of meetings is 2.4 days. Of course, some kinds of meetings, particularly for training, may be much longer (perhaps several weeks) while other kinds may be much shorter (perhaps only two hours).

A meeting's schedule must accommodate program sessions, breaks, and usually meals. Individual sessions typically last about 50 minutes. After two such sessions, attendees should be given a break during which they can stretch, make a quick phone call, or get some refreshments. Breaks can vary from ten minutes (time to grab a cup of coffee) to more formal receptions with fancy refreshments. At least an hour should be allowed for the simplest, most modest meal. Time to set up and break down meeting room configurations or set tables must be allowed. Time must be scheduled to view exhibits, and most meetings that include overnight travel for participants will no doubt schedule free time or group entertainment.

Opening Session

The distance the meeting site is from the majority of participants and the accessibility of transportation will influence opening session time. Some airlines offer special rates for Tuesday through Thursday flights. Most offer special rates for staying at a destination over a Saturday night. (Most attendees do not want a weekend meeting.) Beginning with a 9:00 A.M. session assumes that everyone lives where the meeting is held, has found very early flights, or has arrived the day or evening before.

If the meeting location has been determined, a look at participant profiles will tell how far attendees must travel to get to the meeting. The first meeting activity might be a reception, held the evening before the opening session. This gives those who have arrived a chance to mingle. Keep in mind that this does cost one additional night's lodging. Opening a meeting at noon with a luncheon or at 2:00 P.M. is another possibility.

Timing Program Sessions

One long-winded speaker who takes an extra 20 minutes can throw off the pace of the entire meeting for the rest of the day. Lunch may get cold, or another speaker might become anxious. A chairperson or coordinator should be assigned for each session. This person introduces the speaker, assists with audiovisual equipment, passes out program materials, and signals the speaker when the session is drawing to a close. Some coordinators keep a bell or flash a light on the podium to signal the speaker that his or her time is almost up. Managing sessions is discussed further in Chapter 10.

People attending intensive meetings absorb little material after they have been sitting and listening for six hours. But it is not uncommon to think that eight hours' worth of material can be packed into a day-long meeting. With meals and breaks, that one-day meeting easily turns into two days.

Remember that a meeting is an investment of time and money. Attendees and meeting sponsors want to feel that the meeting is productive. If six hours is needed to accomplish the meeting objectives, then a three-day meeting would dilute the feelings of accomplishment. On the other hand, an excessively short meeting can cause people to feel short-changed.

Remember also that one of the greatest costs to the meeting participant and meeting sponsor is time away from work. For example, when teachers are away from the classroom, substitutes must be hired. Doctors, lawyers, and dentists lose income when they are not in their offices. If a sales representative averages two sales per day and attends a meeting for two days, the company is minus four sales that may be worth thousands of dollars.

Pacing Program Sessions

The participant profiles are very helpful to the meeting planner in setting the pace of the meeting. Even in small decisions, such as the length of coffee breaks, the planner needs to keep in mind who is attending the meeting.

Review the profile of the typical attendee to get insight into the tempo of the meeting. Younger people have shorter attention spans. Therefore, one might try to keep lectures brief and content specific. Older persons may need to move about more often. In that case, frequent breaks might be scheduled or sessions may be held in different rooms so that meeting participants do not just settle into one chair for an entire day.

Other aspects of the participant profile also influence pacing—how far people have traveled to the meeting and whether spouses or companions are present, for example. At some meetings, time must be allowed for managers and sales representatives to check in with their offices. If this is the case, the meeting schedule should take into account differences in time zones. For instance, Californians attending a meeting in New York have no need for an hour-long break at 10:00 A.M. because it is only 7:00 A.M. on the West Coast and their coworkers are unlikely to be in their offices.

The complexity of the material being presented must also be considered. When demanding topics are being covered more breaks and sessions for questions and answers should be included in the program. The meeting planner should look at the program material for clues about pacing the meeting.

A final consideration in pacing a meeting is cost. The meeting planner must once again keep in mind the hidden cost of time away from work, which is quite expensive for some professions. For some groups, the point of a meeting is to immerse themselves in training and sharing information at the lowest cost to themselves in time and money. They may be willing to start their meetings early in the morning and continue with working sessions after dinner. On the other hand, most common interest group meetings have self-pay participants who are willing to pay to develop their hobbies. They might enjoy a slower pace with varied leisure-time activities. The meeting planner should still be sensitive to the costs in time and money that these attendees will incur in order to go to the meeting.

Program Components

Most meetings include four major activities: meeting sessions; food and beverage service; exhibitions and trade shows; and free-time activities. A bare-bones, two-to-three hour meeting may consist of only one or two meeting sessions with a coffee break.

Every program component has a cost. For example, function rooms will usually have a charge. Most properties will waive or reduce these charges if the meeting sponsor also purchases enough room nights. If 300 people attend a four-day meeting, and attendees pay for 1,000 room nights, the hotel might not charge for the meeting rooms. If meals are purchased for the meeting, there may be no room rental charge. Certainly food and beverages cost money. There are costs for audiovisual equipment, and professional speakers and entertainers must be paid. When planning the program, all of these costs must be estimated and a budget established. Registration fees may be set with these costs in mind.

Meeting Sessions

A meeting's working sessions usually include general assemblies, at which everyone meets, and breakout sessions, where groups break away from the entire group for smaller meetings. The ideal meeting program offers both types of sessions. Interest peaks when there is a variety of options. From a physical and psychological standpoint, six hours of general sessions with speakers who simply lecture tends to elicit the meeting planner's most dreaded evaluation response: "Boring."

General Sessions

Certain meeting activities are best handled in general sessions. General sessions include the opening session, which is called the *welcome*. The content of the opening session is one of the most important issues facing the meeting sponsor and meeting planner. If people are meeting to accomplish critical organizational business, a sincere welcome followed by a summary of the task at hand that is delivered by a person in a major leadership position might be most effective. But other meetings will get off to a good start if a professional speaker with an interesting point of view on a subject of general interest addresses the group. In any event, the opening session will set the tone of the meeting, whether it is a day-long workshop or a three-day convention. Therefore, the content of the opening session should be related to the program's theme.

The closing session is often a banquet with presentations and awards. It is important because it gives the final impression of the meeting.

Conducting organizational business, such as electing officers or voting on new bylaws, usually requires that everyone at the meeting be present at a general session. Here, the secretary of the organization may read the minutes from the last meeting. The treasurer might give a report. Sometimes a quorum of an association's membership is required for a binding vote on organizational business.

Keynote speakers customarily address a general session or assembly. And there may well be other reasons to request that all meeting participants attend a general session; for example, to introduce a new product or a new organizational leader.

Breakout Sessions

For educational purposes—training or sharing information—smaller breakout sessions are more suitable than general assemblies. A smaller group absorbs information easier and smaller rooms give a visual advantage. For example, after an opening session at which a general subject or theme is discussed, participants may be able to choose between three breakout sessions on topics related to the general subject or theme. These breakout sessions can be repeated several times over the course of the meeting so that all attendees have a chance to attend them.

Breakout sessions might also be called *workshops* or *roundtables*. Holding a workshop implies that a skill will be taught and practiced. Roundtables are usually held for small groups whose task is to exchange ideas on a particular topic. But on many meeting program schedules, breakout sessions are simply listed as "Session 1," "Session 2," and so forth, or they may be designated by the topic to which they relate (for example, "Budget Session").

Finding Speakers

Whether to pay a speaker must be decided. Some people make their living giving speeches, and they have predetermined fees. Other speakers would probably consider it an honor to speak to the group at no cost. Usually a speaker's expenses, such as travel and lodging, are covered, and often a gift or honorarium is given.

When trying to come up with a suitable speaker at no charge, be creative. Satisfied customers of a business or those who have gained from an association membership can be successful speakers by giving worthwhile testimonies. Members with hobbies that coincide with the business or association can often provide fascinating speeches. Amateur talent can be found in many groups holding meetings. This talent can be a good source of education or entertainment. The local Convention and Visitors Bureau often is happy to provide a speaker to welcome the group to the city or area.

Perhaps a civil servant's expertise would provide valuable information to an organization's membership. Government agencies do not generally charge for public speaking, and there may be some agency that either controls or affects some aspect of the organization. For example, the Internal Revenue Service might provide a speaker for certified public accountants on recent tax law revisions. A state parks department employee might provide valuable information to a meeting of naturalists.

As noted, a professional speaker or personality might be retained to deliver the keynote address or other speeches. These individuals might be political representatives, well known authors, or show business celebrities. Famous speakers can command over $25,000 for one appearance. Speakers bureaus and talent managers are more than happy to make suggestions for professional speakers who might be appropriate for a given meeting.

Professional speakers demand expenses, including transportation, accommodations, food, and incidental costs. Occasionally, money can be saved by piggybacking with a speaker's other appearances. Transportation to a meeting site could be shared by two different audiences. Contracts with professional speakers should be very detailed. They should spell out time, place, fees, expenses paid, audiovisual equipment needs, rehearsal requirements, security provisions, and provisions for cancellations. It is usually worth the expense to have an experienced attorney draft or review these contracts before they are signed.

Between the speaker who just donates his or her time and the five-figure–fee speaker is a vast choice. Many people who are experts in a particular field hold seminars as their primary source of income. Their fees range from $100 to $1,000 per hour. These people can provide résumés and references (which should be double-checked). Ideally, the meeting planner sees a videotape of a speaker before signing a contract for the person's services.

Methods of Presentation

General and breakout sessions can be presented in various ways. Some presentations are more active than others, meaning that they require participants to do more than just sit and listen. In a program, a mix of presentations is the ideal.

❏ **Speeches.** Many general sessions typically involve speeches. Some meetings feature a keynote speaker. Other meeting sessions will also involve one person addressing the group. In these cases, meeting participants are simply receiving information. Remember that sitting and listening are relatively passive activities. Unless they are actively engaged in a question-and-answer session or working on brief projects with their neighbors, participants are only responding to what they see and hear.

The dummy program should show which sessions will include speeches. It is not necessary to list who will be giving speeches at this time unless the speaker's availability has already been confirmed or unless the speaker's presentation is the one program component on which the rest of the meeting depends.

Speakers may be chosen by an organizing committee, the organization's officers, session coordinators, or possibly by the meeting planner. Choosing speakers is one of the most delicate decisions of the meeting planning process, and it can make or break a meeting. For larger meetings of associations and businesses, the president or chief executive officer is usually the one who oversees the meeting. Often, this is the person who welcomes and closes the meeting. For smaller meetings such as workshops, clinics, or retreats, a person representing the meeting's sponsor or the person who will be training the participants may be asked to give welcoming or concluding remarks.

Usually, a keynote speaker delivers the final message—announcing news, reviewing the meeting, or reiterating central ideas that were discussed. The keynote speech might be inspirational, sending people off to sell more goods, build a better product, or raise more money. The keynote speaker should be dynamic.

Though not as effective, a speaker can be videotaped and the tape shown at the meeting. Somewhat more effective is live transmission of a speaker.

Speakers should be sent several forms including an audiovisual needs form as shown in Figure 4.1. Chapter 9 includes a sample audiovisual equipment contract. Chapter 10 gives more information about costs for speakers and audiovisual equipment and specifications. Include a taping or proceedings release form if these are part of the meeting. A form to confirm transportation and accommodation needs is also sent to speakers. Chapter 12 includes a sample of this form. The Speaker Checklist on page 48 reminds the planner of speaker obligations.

❑ **Special Events and Audiovisual Presentations.** Certain meeting sessions can take on the aura of a prime time television spectacular. Their aim is to excite the meeting participants about a product, a person, or an idea. Certainly the presentations themselves are exciting! Dancers, singers, and role playing can all be a part of the presentation. There are companies whose business it is to put together special events for meetings. One might work with a talent or booking agent to incorporate this kind of entertainment. Needless to say, these presentations are quite expensive. Music and scripts may have to be written, actors and actresses hired, and costumes and props manufactured.

Audiovisual presentations are more commonly employed than special

---

Speaker _____

Title _____

Affiliation _____

Address _____

City/State/ZIP _____

Work Ph. (   ) _____ **Fax (   )** _____ **Home Ph. (   )** _____

Please check off the equipment you need for your presentation and describe any particular requirements.

❑ Table lectern _____   ❑ Stand-up lectern _____
❑ Flip chart/easel/markers _____   ❑ Board/chalk/markers _____
❑ Videotape player _____   ❑ Tape size _____
❑ 35mm slide projector _____   ❑ Overhead projector _____
❑ Motion picture projector _____   ❑ Film size _____
❑ Other _____
❑ Remarks _____

Figure 4.1 **Audiovisual Equipment Needs Form**

events. Twenty years ago, using two side projectors was considered innovative. Today with videotapes, back-lit screens, and a myriad of electronic technology, audiovisual productions are very elaborate. Once again, there are many companies that specialize in audiovisual presentations. Hiring these companies adds to the cost of the meeting.

❑ **Panels.** Panels can be used in breakout sessions or general sessions. Here, three or four speakers, often representing different points of view, discuss a topic. A debate can be staged between speakers representing opposite points of view. Panel presentations may also be effective in meetings at which groups that have collaborated on a project want to report their findings.

Panels encourage audience participation. The effectiveness of a panel depends on the panelists. If one panelist is a poor speaker, it will most likely be overlooked if the other panelists are better presenters The general format of a panel presentation is for each panelist to make a statement and then invite questions. A moderator should be appointed to ensure that all panelists get to speak and that their interplay with the audience is smooth.

❑ **Small Group Interchange.** Another successful, active means of presenting a session is to divide meeting participants into small working groups that are given a problem to solve. The results of each group's efforts are then discussed among the session participants.

An example is budgeting for an advertising campaign. The groups are told that there is $100,000 to be spent on advertising a product. Each group then brainstorms how to allocate the money on different forms of advertising. A corporation that wishes to solve a problem such as excessive absenteeism might assign groups to come up with ideas for encouraging attendance.

Small groups can also be used to prioritize organizational activities and aims. They can be used to iron out details of the organization's structure (for example, a new set of bylaws) or to simply gather information about organizational trends and challenges.

❑ **Computer-Assisted Interaction.** Probably the newest method of holding meeting sessions is using computers for interaction between participants and facilitator, speaker, or session chair. One or two attendees might sit in front of a computer terminal and actively participate in learning a skill, such as using a new computer program. In more sophisticated cases, participants communicate directly with the session leader via computer.

If an organization is facing an especially touchy problem or if meeting participants are reluctant to publicly express their opinions, a computer can be used to anonymously solicit solutions. "Why are sales off 30 percent this quarter?" "What do you think we could do to improve your day-to-day working conditions?" Each meeting attendee keys in his or her thoughts. The session leader can then report the group's ideas. Bear in mind that planning for computer-assisted interaction greatly affects where a meeting can be held.

Food and Beverage Service

Food and beverage service plays an integral part of most meetings, although some meetings do not include meals, coffee breaks, or receptions in their formal programs. For now, the meeting planner must decide whether food and beverage service is necessary, figure the approximate length of time needed, and schedule it in the program. The number of meals included in the program dramatically affects the cost of the meeting. Chapter 11 discusses food and beverage management and deals extensively with meal setup and menu choices.

Coffee Breaks

If a meeting lasts more than two hours, some kind of break for refreshments is usually expected. Two coffee breaks are usually offered at longer meetings. Soft drinks may be offered at afternoon breaks. These breaks must be taken into account in making up a dummy program. A rule of thumb is that attendees should be given a ten-minute break every hour or so.

The length of a break will depend on the number of participants at the meeting. Serving refreshments to a large group takes more time than for a smaller group. Some meetings discourage bringing food and drink back to the meeting sessions.

Sometimes a coffee bar remains open throughout the day; attendees can help themselves whenever they wish. The refreshments may be set to the side in a room where attendees are already meeting or a separate room may be reserved where attendees can enjoy a beverage and perhaps a light snack. The coffee/soft drink service might also include food. Sweet rolls in the morning and cookies or fruit in the afternoon are popular choices. Chapter 11 discusses breaks in more detail.

The meeting planner should consider finding a sponsor to underwrite the cost of the breaks if possible. For example, if law librarians are meeting, a company that distributes software for legal research or a company that publishes legal books might be glad for the goodwill that such exposure brings. A notice in the meeting program or a sign on the refreshment table is an appropriate way to acknowledge a sponsor.

Meals

Time for meals, breakfast, lunch, and dinner must be allowed for in planning the program of a meeting. It doesn't matter whether the meal is part of the program or if attendees eat on their own—the time must still be scheduled.

Meals do lend themselves to being combined with other meeting activities such as listening to a speaker or even viewing an exhibition. On the other hand, some people prefer that meals not include any formal meeting activity. Meals provide time for participants to socialize, but a great deal of business is carried out informally between attendees during the meal breaks at meetings.

❏ **Breakfast.** Meeting planners debate about whether or not to offer breakfast as a part of the program. When breakfast is offered and included in the price of the meeting, attendance at breakfast is low because many people prefer breakfast in their rooms. More and more properties are offering room service breakfast as part of the room price; thus breakfast is not included on the program. When a continental breakfast (coffee, fruit juice, and a sweet roll) is offered, one can count on many attendees arriving at the end of the time scheduled for the breakfast.

❏ **Lunch.** More lunches are served at meetings than any other meal, aside from breaks. It is best to keep the attendees at the meeting property if there are morning and afternoon sessions.

❏ **Dinner.** Sometimes the meeting sponsor provides the evening meal and sometimes meeting participants are free to eat on their own. A closing banquet is the tradition at many meetings, especially at lengthier or more elaborate meetings.

During very intensive meetings, participants may benefit by getting away from the meeting environment. Taking them to another site, perhaps a local restaurant, for the meal can be refreshing. Of course, transportation has to be taken into consideration in planning meals away from the meeting property.

Receptions

Receptions or cocktail buffets are often part of a meeting program. They can be held in conjunction with an exhibition or be sponsored by an organization other than the meeting sponsor. If more formal attire is required at a reception, an hour should be set aside after the last meeting session for attendees to change and relax. The reception itself should not last for more than an hour. See Chapter 11 for more information about receptions.

Exhibitions and Trade Shows

Sufficient time must be scheduled to view an exhibition or trade show that is held in conjunction with the meeting. If the exhibition is combined with another program component, such as a luncheon, the time allotted for that program component should be extended. As the scope of exhibitions and the price that companies have paid to exhibit expands, so does the amount of time allowed for viewing increase. If the exhibition is held in a place other than the meeting property, transportation time must be taken into consideration. Exhibitions are discussed more fully in Chapter 3.

Free-Time Activities

After figuring the minimum amount of time needed to hold meeting sessions, meals, coffee breaks, and receptions, the meeting planner should assess the participants' need for free time. A rule of thumb is to give meeting participants one full morning or afternoon off for every three days of meetings. The participant profile will again be a guide to what is appropriate for the group as a whole, and the meeting's objectives will provide useful information in this regard. For example, a group of travel agents will probably want time to explore the locality in which its meeting is held in order to be able to make recommendations to travelers about local accommodations and attractions. A group of senior-level managers from an international corporation may treat their meeting as a very business-like affair—they may not care to visit that world-class museum that is a block from the hotel where they are meeting.

Because many people write off the cost of meetings as a business expense, the meeting planner should be aware of Internal Revenue Service regulations regarding business expenses. The IRS is strict in measuring the amount of free time against working time in deciding whether to allow deductions for business expenses. Figure 4.2 reprints the regulation.

A phrase frequently seen in tour brochures is *afternoon at leisure*. If you are on a vacation package tour, this means that nothing is scheduled for that afternoon. If you are at a meeting, it means you finally get a break and can visit the town, call the home office, or just relax.

Tours of the convention city are logical free-time activities, especially if the meeting attendees are not from the area. The meeting planner can either organize the tour or provide information on making reservations with a local tour operator to the attendees. Side trips out of the convention city can also be planned. A half-day trip to Pike's Peak for attendees at a con-

---

[Sec. 274]

SEC 274. DISALLOWANCE OF CERTAIN ENTERTAINMENT, ETC., EXPENSES.

[Sec. 274(a)]

(a) ENTERTAINMENT, AMUSEMENT, OR RECREATION.—

(1) IN GENERAL.—No deduction otherwise allowable under this chapter shall be allowed for any item—

(A) ACTIVITY.—With respect to an activity which is of a type generally considered to constitute entertainment, amusement, or recreation, unless the taxpayer establishes that the item was directly related to, or, in the case of an item directly preceding or following a substantial and bona fide business discussion (including business meetings at a convention or otherwise), that such item was associated with, the active conduct of the taxpayer's trade or business, or

(B) FACILITY.—With respect to a facility used in connection with an activity referred to in subparagraph (A).

Figure 4.2 **Internal Revenue Code Regulation Regarding Deduction of Meeting Expenses**

vention in Denver, visiting parks or museums, or going to shopping outlets are examples of side trips.

Going to plays, seeing preforming artists, and attending concerts are other options for free-time activities. Although after-dinner speakers are not popular, after-dinner *entertainment* is often desirable.

Sports and recreation provide excellent free-time activities. The group might be taken to watch a sporting event or participate in some sport. If the meeting is held at a resort, swimming, golf, and tennis facilities are usually available to attendees. Note, however, that the resort may charge fees to the attendees who wish to use these facilities. Dividing the group into teams and running a sports tournament provides structured free-time activity. Chapter 12 gives further information about free-time activities, companion programs, and pre- and post-meeting tours.

Free-time activities can add great expense to a meeting. When considering them as program components, determine if they will be optional, for an extra charge or if their costs will be included in the registration fee.

The program will change several times. Speakers may be unable to attend, an outside organization may volunteer to host a meal, and 30 additional attendees may unexpectedly register, but most often the general time blocks will remain the same as those you've designed.

SPEAKER CHECKLIST

Name of speaker _____

Name of coordinator _____

Day and date of speech _____

Time scheduled for speech _____

Objectives of speech _____

Title of presentation _____

A/V needs _____

Travel needs _____

    Date arriving: _____

    Date departing: _____

    Air reservations made: _____

    Housing arranged: _____

Security needs _____

Rehearsal set _____

Bio received _____

Tape/proceedings release received _____

Handouts received for reproduction _____

CHAPTER ACTIVITIES

4

The Association of Jacuzzi Contractors is holding its three-day annual meeting. Cleveland has been selected as the site. Approximately 300 people from 40 different states will attend. Sixty-five percent of the attendees will be males aged 30–60 years old. Most own their own businesses, and their income is $40,000–70,000 per year. They will self-pay for the conference, and 50 percent of them will bring their spouses to the meeting.

Determine what kinds of sessions and presentation methods are best for the meeting objectives and how long sessions should last. Then prepare a dummy program for a meeting based on the following information and using the forms provided.

Objective	Type of Session	Presentation Method	Estimated Time Required
Explain new installation methods			
Elect new board of directors			
Update on demographics (who buys jacuzzis)			
Rewrite bylaws			
Honor outgoing president			
Show new products			
Review successful marketing efforts			
Future association outlook			
Announce chemical pigment research			
Free-time activity			

Now chart the dummy program:

Day 1	Session	Presentation Method	Number Expected
9:00			
15			
30			
45			
10:00			
15			
30			
45			
11:00			
15			
30			
45			
12:00			
15			
30			
45			
1:00			
15			
30			
45			
2:00			
15			
30			
45			
3:00			
15			
30			
45			
4:00			
15			
30			
45			
5:00			
15			
30			
45			

Day 1	Session	Presentation Method	Number Expected
6:00			
15			
30			
45			
7:00			
15			
30			
45			
8:00			

5

Site Selection

Upon completion of this chapter, you will be able to:

1. Determine appropriate sites for the size and type of the meeting

2. Weigh the merits of different sites depending on season, climate, and political considerations

3. Evaluate the accessibility of different meeting sites

4. Assess sites according to membership, leisure-time preferences, and special needs

The ring of a cash register and the zip-zip of a credit card imprinter are sounds that accompany meetings. A conference attendee is a very desirable visitor to any locale.

Most cities have a Convention and Visitors Bureau (CVB) that serves as the nucleus of efforts to promote its area as a convention site. A CVB's membership includes hotels, motels, restaurants, transportation companies, and attractions. When considering a city as a meeting site, a call to its CVB is often a first step. A city's Chamber of Commerce might serve as the CVB or Destination Marketing Organization (DMO).

Convention participants spend more money than average pleasure travellers; thus, they are considered "quality" visitors. They are preferred over the "day visitor" trade. In the most recent survey conducted by the International Assoc. of Convention and Visitor Bureaus, the average spending in a U.S. city for a convention delegate was $573 and for a trade-show delegate, was $866.

It isn't surprising that the economic meat and potatoes of many hotels, motels, and resort properties is meetings. A hotel's income often depends on group sales, so hotels are very willing to advertise themselves as excellent sites for conferences and conventions. An irresistible offer from a property can cause it to be selected as a meeting site on the spot with no further investigation of alternatives.

Many associations and businesses do not go through the agony of choosing a meeting site. They are invited and wooed by cities and convention centers. Many times, incentives such as price concessions or free receptions are attractive, but the meeting planner still has to determine if the location meets the needs of the group. Local attractions also entice convention business by offering group discounts, and restaurants might offer discount coupons.

When is a site decision made? Conventions of over 100 attendees usually choose a site at last a year in advance. Often the next meeting dates and location are announced at the conclusion of an earlier meeting. Thus, a meeting planner spends a great deal of time organizing a current meeting and at the same time negotiating a future meeting. For large organizations, the meeting site is set five or six years in advance. Sometimes a site is selected with the anticipation that a convention center or additional hotel rooms will be constructed.

Major Considerations

Some details about an organization are givens. Choosing a site for a meeting is controlled to some degree by these fixed considerations. Some of these factors can be used to focus on places that are appropriate for the meeting or they may provide a means of eliminating certain locations.

Meeting Size

The size of the meeting—that is, number of participants expected—is so important that it is one of the first considerations of planning a meeting. By looking at the total membership of the organization and the history of its meetings, an estimate of the number of attendees can be made. The size of an exhibition may also affect site selection.

For small- and medium-sized meetings, size is not of importance in geographical site selection. It is with large associations and businesses that the size of a meeting immediately eliminates certain locations. A national convention of the American Medical Association cannot be accommodated in the Black Hills of South Dakota, no matter how beautiful or historically significant that area is. Only a few cities can accommodate the national conventions of political parties, labor unions, or fraternal organizations.

The key point is how many hotel rooms are available and where they are located in a city. For very large meetings, attendees are housed throughout the city in several different properties. Therefore, there must be enough suitable rooms available and accessible transportation between the properties and the convention center or meeting site.

Figure 5.1 shows which cities hosted the most meetings in 1986 and the number of hotel rooms available within a 30-minute drive.

Just as a large number of attendees eliminates certain locations, so can the need for exhibition or trade show space exclude certain cities. If a 200,000 square foot exhibit accompanies the meeting, then the location

City	Number of conventions[1]	Number of hotel rooms[2]
Leading Convention Cities, 1986		
1. Dallas	2,090	37,601
2. Atlanta	1,470	35,000
3. New Orleans	1,000	26,000
4. New York	971	100,000[3]
5. San Antonio	954	16,000
6. Washington	857	47,000
7. Sacramento	856	2,500
8. St. Louis	782	20,000
9. Houston	727	36,000
10. Chicago	690	40,000

(1) Convention figures represent those held within city limits of city convention bureau designations. (2) Within 30-minute drive of downtown. (3) Within city.

Source: Advertising Age

Figure 5.1 **Leading Convention Cities**

choice is narrowed considerably. Only a few cities have a civic center or convention center that will accommodate an exhibition of that size.

Figure 5.2 shows the ten largest convention centers in North America and the square footage available for trade shows.

Organizational Characteristics

No site selection is necessary if an organization always holds its meeting at the same place. Delta Airlines is an example. It originated as a crop-dusting service in Monroe, Louisiana, and its annual meeting is always held there. Other organizations always hold their meetings in their headquarters city. Certain sites will be predetermined for special reasons. For example, a company president might be retiring and the annual meeting will be held in his or her hometown in honor of the retirement.

Some organizations pick a limited number of sites and rotate their meetings through them. Once again, the size of the meeting might be the reason. An organization may only have a few options for cities that can accommodate its meetings.

Many organizations move their meetings around the country on a regular basis. This tends to even out the financial strain for members traveling from organizations with memberships from throughout the nation. An east coast resident knows that cross-country air fare will not have to be budgeted for every year. The Society of Travel and Tourism Educators, whose members are from the United States and Canada, follows such a rotation pattern. One year the meeting site was Wilmington, Delaware (east coast). The next year it was New Orleans, Louisiana (mid-continent). The following year the convention site was Long Beach, California (west coast).

City	Exh/mtg sq. ft.
Chicago	1,600,000
Houston	1,296,000
Las Vegas	1,100,000
New York	780,000
Detroit	700,000
Atlanta	640,000
Dallas	600,000
Denver	500,000
San Diego	450,000
Atlantic City	436,000
Philadelphia	435,000
Anaheim	420,000

Source: Copyright © 1990 by CMP Publications, Inc., 600 Community Drive, Mannhasset, NY 11030. Reprinted from Business Travel NEWS with permission.

Figure 5.2 **Largest North American Convention Centers**

Site selection patterns narrow down the geographical grid of where a meeting is to be held. The planner, for example, only looks at east coast cities when the pattern indicates so.

The type of organization holding the meeting obviously influences site selection. For example, a conservative religious group is not going to meet in Las Vegas, Nevada, or in Atlantic City, New Jersey, where the social atmospheres and entertainment options conflict with the group's stated philosophy.

Certain organizations have special needs that affect site selection. For example, many educational groups prefer to meet at a university or in a school setting. Some scientific organizations need to have access to laboratories. In selecting a location for a meeting, these needs might either eliminate certain sites or bring to mind logical locations for the meeting.

The type of meeting and its objective may eliminate certain sites. A workshop utilizing computers will not be held on a remote island where electrical service is unreliable. A retreat where attendees are to gain personal insight and introspection would probably not be held in downtown Manhattan. On the other hand, some locations, such as Ft. Lauderdale, Florida, are natural choices for meetings that are held strictly for pleasure.

Analyzing the type of participant or the profile of the typical attendee is extremely helpful in deciding on the site of the meeting. The Antique Maserati Owners with their expensive hobby and high disposable incomes, would not be enthusiastic about meeting in a small midwestern town. They would prefer the glitz of a big city or the luxury of a resort area. Though the typing teachers might prefer a little glitz, since their meeting is strictly educational, their expectations of a meeting site would not include glamour. Nor does the costs of the glitzy location suit their budgets or travel allowances.

Transportation and Accessibility

Essential to site selection is transportation and accessibility. There must be adequate transportation to the meeting site and adequate transportation for participants during the meeting.

Meetings may draw attendees from the state or region or throughout the nation. A regional meeting will have more people arriving in autos. At larger national meetings, attendees will primarily fly in.

An example of a site with transportation problems is a small island off the coast of an eastern seaboard state to which one eight-passenger plane makes two round trips daily. Attendees are virtually held captive by the plane schedule. If this is the most desirable meeting location, however, the meeting planner may make other transportation arrangements.

If a meeting is so large that participants are spread out in several hotels within an area and must get to the host property or civic center for meeting sessions, then choosing a site with public transportation and available parking is essential. Renting shuttle buses to run between major properties is an alternative. Transportation management is discussed in Chapter 12.

Certain meetings, particularly retreats, may be designed to contain the membership at a remote location with few disturbances from the outside world. In this case, the site is chosen with that in mind and transportation may not be considered a major need.

Timing

Time and place are intertwined. A city may have to be eliminated from the site search if many meetings are being held there at once or if the costs for attending are inflated because of the tourist season. In addition, the days of the week for which the meeting is scheduled and its proximity to a holiday may be factors.

❑ **Day of the week.**   Whether to hold a meeting during the week or over a weekend is always a debate. For business meetings, participants don't want to give up weekend time for work. Yet in commercial centers, weekend hotel rates are much less expensive than weekday rates. Rooms are filled with business travellers Monday through Thursday. On the other hand, weekend rates are at a peak at resorts, casino hotels, or attraction areas. Sleeping room and transportation costs are affected by which days of the week are chosen for the meeting.

❑ **Holidays.**   Many sites are very amenable to hosting meetings over certain holidays when they would not otherwise book many visitors, but most groups avoid having meetings during holiday periods and over long weekends. People want their holiday time for personal or family commitments. Common interest groups or ethnic groups may be exceptions to this, but the smart meeting planner will not make assumptions about this.

❑ **Events.**   The timing of other events can eliminate certain cities from the choosing process. Hotels may be totally booked, and the event can also be a distraction for serious meetings. If a meeting is to be held in the first or second week of October, it cannot be accommodated in Annapolis, Maryland. That is when the Sail and Power Boat Shows are held and accommodations in town are impossible to obtain. Most groups avoid New Orleans during Mardi Gras for similar reasons.

❑ **Season or climate.**   If recreation and sightseeing are slated for the meeting program, then the seasonality of a site is a factor. Obviously, warmer southern sites are desired in winter, as are ski resorts. A more exotic location might be affordable during the off-season. For example, San Juan, Puerto Rico, is a bargain in June. Quebec is lovely, and prices there are lower in October.

Severe weather conditions make certain sites chancy as meeting locations during certain times of the year. A city that routinely suffers winter blizzards may not be a good choice for a January meeting for which most attendees will fly in. Certainly a good portion of the North America could be eliminated as a meeting site from June to September if tornadoes are a fear.

Figure 5.3 shows the most popular months for meetings.

Cost

The participant profile, which shows average participant income, might rule out locations such as Honolulu, Hawaii, because of the high cost of meeting there. Some cities have higher costs of living than others. St. Louis, Missouri, is reasonably priced, while New York City is extremely expensive. Though New York or San Francisco seem to be perfect meeting cities, the costs that a meeting participant would have to incur while there might be prohibitive. The meeting planner must carefully calculate average costs for such items as air travel, ground transportation, lodging, and meals in determining whether a meeting site is a sensible choice in terms of cost.

When planning government meetings, costs have to be factored differently. With few exceptions, government employees are given per diems that reflect the cost of living of the areas in which their meetings are held. These per diems are expected to cover lodging, taxes, meals, and incidentals. Transportation to the site and often meeting registration (which may include some meals) is usually paid directly in addition to per diem. Examples of these per diems are Philadelphia, $113 per day; Phoenix, $83; and Boston, $121. Figure 5.4 shows a per diem allowance chart for some meeting sites in North America.

Some locations have taxes that fall disproportionately on travelers and visitors. These usually take the form of hotel room taxes. In July 1989, the hotel tax in Washington, D.C., was 11 percent. Restaurant and rental cars also may have local taxes or "add ons." These can be as high as nine percent. Nonprofit organizations may be tax exempt, allowing city taxes to be waived.

Free-Time Activities

As mentioned in Chapter 3, some groups expect sports, energetic night life, or spectacular sightseeing opportunities.

Months Meetings Held

Dec–Feb	11%
Mar–May	32%
Jun–Aug	25%
Sep–Nov	26%

Source: M. Concorso, The Meetings Market '90, Meetings & Conventions Magazine/Reed Travel Group.

Figure 5.3 **Most Popular Months for Meetings**

City	Amount
New York	$147
Los Angeles	120
Chicago	123
Denver	99
Dallas	108
Kansas City	86

Figure 5.4 **Federal Government Per Diem Allowances for Representative North American Meeting Sites**

The type of organization that is holding the meeting can suggest free-time activities. For example, archaeologists might appreciate Williamsburg, Virginia, which is near the Jamestown excavations, or a meeting location near Indian cliff dwellings. Site selection for meetings held strictly for pleasure can offer numerous and varied site options: beach resorts, casino cities, winter sports communities, spas, national parks, and monuments.

More and more meeting participants are accompanied by their spouses or companions. In light of this, a meeting site should have recreational and sightseeing activities in which these guests can participate while meeting sessions are being held.

Certain meetings are self-contained, with all activities taking place within a property. Other meetings rely on a location's other attractions to provide food service, entertainment, and shopping. For example, if the meeting does not provide group meals, restaurants in a city must be evaluated. For many people, shopping is a means of recreation; if this is the case for participants and companions, the meeting planner should be aware of whether the city has a distinct commercial area and whether a range of goods is available to suit participants' budgets.

Pre- and post-convention tours can have some bearing on where a meeting is held. Many oversees meetings have optional tours. The American Society of Travel Agents holds its meetings in faraway places such as Budapest. Literally dozens of pre- and post-convention tours are organized. As for domestic meetings, who's to say that after a convention in Denver, an extra day to see Pike's Peak and the Air Force Academy would not be appealing? Similarly, Niagara Falls would be a fitting post-tour from a meeting in Toronto.

Additional Considerations

If several sites are appropriate in light of tradition, timing, size, transportation, costs, and free-time expectations, then other considerations are taken into account.

❑ **Outside Contractors.** The locality in which a meeting is held has to have resources to meet the needs of attendees. Ground transportation, tour operators, and audiovisual companies with recording, transcription, and translation capabilities may be necessary. Florists, decorators, staging, costuming, and entertainment providers are other outside contractors that may be essential.

❑ **Image.** The image of a city can influence its standing in site selection. For example, Washington, D.C., has a high rate of street crime, which might eliminate it as a meeting site for some groups. The meeting planner must research whether a locality's reputation or image would negatively affect holding a successful meeting at the site.

Some cities have a reputation of being friendly. The citizens of Atlanta and Houston exude Southern hospitality. On the other hand, a city might have a reputation of being cool or unfriendly to tourists. Even though some of these perceptions are stereotypes that can be contradicted by facts or experiences, they will influence a potential participant's willingness to attend a meeting at a certain location.

❑ **Outside Assistance.** It is always pleasant to feel wanted. Offers of assistance or extensions of services for a meeting might be the deciding factor in choosing a site. Often the members of a national organization's local chapter or the employees of a regional office of a large corporation might extend an invitation for the meeting to be held in their home city. These local members or employees usually offer to take on various meeting planning duties. The local organization might volunteer to sponsor a reception or meal or might help in convincing area dignitaries to attend functions of the meeting.

As mentioned, Chambers of Commerce and CVBs extend invitations to groups to meet in their city. States, through their offices of tourism and development, also participate in the invitation process for large conventions. The assistance that these groups offer might be providing printed material on the area or providing "giveaways." For example, Atlanta might donate pins or tote bags imprinted with its dogwood blossom emblem. The Chamber of Commerce might offer to host a reception, maintain a hospitality suite, or transport VIPs. Some CVBs even offer personnel to help with meeting registration or will process a meeting's registration through its office. The CVB might be in a position to offer reduced rates for the rental of the civic center and to help with multiproperty reservations.

International Sites

Should the meeting be held at an international or domestic location? If the organization has international membership, the world presents many site choices. Most meetings are held where the business or organization is headquartered, but many groups look at overseas locations. For American travelers, the Caribbean, Canada, and Mexico are generally accessible and reasonably priced.

Three considerations take on more importance when choosing international sites. First, transportation accessibility for the meeting participants must be carefully considered when contemplating an overseas meeting. Second, can the organization's members or the business's employees afford the time and cost of travel? Can enough people attend to make the meeting worthwhile and ensure that meeting objectives are met? Third, budget considerations take on more importance for the meeting organization due to fluctuations in the value of the dollar overseas.

In an effort to balance the trade deficit, federal tax laws are very strict concerning tax write-offs for attending international meetings. Before considering an international site, a meeting planner must become knowledgeable about these restrictions. For tax purposes, international meetings are considered to be those held outside of North America, defined as the United States, Canada, Mexico, U.S. holdings in the Caribbean, and the South Pacific. Other Caribbean countries are included from time to time in this list, depending on current diplomatic and economic relations. The U.S. State Department can advise a planner on which countries are exempt from tax restrictions.

For international meetings, documents must be submitted to the government that show, among other things, the program of the meeting and the nationality of the organization's membership. Proof must be submitted that the meeting itself is related to the attendee's business or trade. To be reimburseable, only one-third of the attendee's time can be not related to business. Only two international meetings may be written off per year. A portion of the tax law is shown in Figure 5.5.

Political climate is a concern when planning international meetings. China in 1990 was an example. Many meetings were scheduled there when its revolution broke out. Though transportation and labor difficulties were solved in a relatively short time, most meetings were cancelled. Often attendees' political opinions can induce them to boycott a meeting in certain places. South Africa and some Central American countries are current examples of locations where an organization's membership may not want to spend its money.

A country's propensity to labor problems and strikes is also a concern in planning international meetings. A strike by bus drivers or taxicab drivers can cause nightmares for a meeting planner. Some countries are known to be more hospitable to visitors than others.

Cruise ships are an alternative to the traditional sites (e.g., hotels, resorts) for a meeting. Once again, tax laws must be reviewed. Currently, if tax write-offs are to be available for meetings held on cruise ships, the ship must be registered in the United States and must stop at U.S. ports. This limits the accessibility of using a cruise ship as a meeting site, since there are few cruises that meet these criteria.

(h) ATTENDANCE AT CONVENTIONS, ETC.—

(1) IN GENERAL.—In the case of any individual who attends a convention, seminar, or similar meeting which is held outside the North American area, no deduction shall be allowed under section 162 for expenses allocable to such meeting unless the taxpayer establishes that the meeting is directly related to the active conduct of his trade or business that, after taking into account in the manner provided by regulations prescribed by the Secretary—

(A) the purpose of such meeting nd the activities taking place at such meeting,

(B) the purposes and activities of the sponsoring organization or groups,

(C) the residences of the active members of the sponsoring organization and the places at which other meetings of the sponsoring organization or groups have been held or will be held, and

(D) such other relevant factors as the taxpayer may present,

it is as reasonable for the meeting to be held outside the North American area as within the North American area.

Figure 5.5 **Internal Revenue Code Regulation on Deduction of Expenses for Meetings Held Outside North America**

International meeting management is much more complex than domestic meeting management, and it presents unique problems. The meeting planner is dealing across long distances, often with non–English-speaking people with different customs and business practices. International meeting planning is a specialty. Usually, tour operators can be employed to assist.

Yes, choosing a place for a meeting is complicated. It includes both gathering factual data and making judgment calls. If a geographical site has been narrowed down to two or three possible locations, the final step is to review and rate the site selection considerations on the following checklist.

SITE SELECTION CHECKLIST

Regional pattern _____

Organizational tradition _____

Meeting needs (e.g., convention center, college laboratory) _____

Participant-type restrictions _____

(To evaluate two or more cities, rank each of the following factors on a 1 to 5 scale, 5 being superior.)

_____ There is adequate number of hotel rooms

     _____ Number in a single property _____

     _____ In how many multiple properties _____   Total # rooms _____

_____ There is adequate exhibit space

     _____ Sq. footage within properties

     _____ Sq. footage within Civic center

_____ Transportation to the site is available via (list carriers) _____

_____

_____ Transfers (airport to possible properties used) available

     _____ Takes how long?

_____ Public transportation at the site is adequate

_____ The timing of the meeting does not interfere with other events

_____ The cost of living is within participants' range

_____ There are recreation and sightseeing possibilities

     List: _____

_____ Special needs can be provided

_____ Needed contractors are available

_____ Adequate food service

_____ Adequate shopping

_____ The city solicits meeting business

_____ The CVB is geared up to assist meetings through providing (check support provided)

     _____ Invitation letters

     _____ Destination brochures

     _____ Destination giveaways

     _____ Multiple property hotel registration

     _____ Registration personnel

     _____ Airport welcome host

     _____ Hotel information and/or greeter

     _____ Hosted reception

     _____ Media support

_____ Local members are available and willing to assist

_____ The city's reputation for friendliness

_____ The city has a low crime rate

_____ The atmosphere of the site is conducive to the type meeting

_____ **Total Score**

5

CHAPTER ACTIVITIES

1. On the checklist, rate your hometown and another city with which you are familiar as a potential meeting site for a national convention.

   Hometown:

   Other City:

2. Look at the participant profiles in Chapter 2 and list five potential meetings sites for:

   The Antique Maserati Owners

   The Teachers of Typing

   The Mutual Insurance Northeast Regional Sales Force

   Explain your suggestions:

Property Selection

Upon completion of this chapter, you will be able to:

1. Narrow down property choices due to size, cost, and location

2. Judge the efficiency of operations of a property

3. Measure the quality of service at a property

4. Carry out meaningful site inspections

S uppose that a site has been selected for the meeting. The next step is to choose a property—a hotel, resort, convention center, or other facility—where the meeting sessions will be held and where the participants will be lodged. Often, site selection and property selection occur at the same time. A meeting planner will rarely invest the time it takes to thoroughly evaluate a meeting site without some assurance that there is a suitable property in the vicinity.

Sometimes choosing a property is simple. An association may want to hold its convention at a time when there is an abundance of meeting space and hotel rooms in the city in which the convention is to be held. Or if a corporation customarily holds an executive retreat at a particular resort, the corporation may have a standing reservation with the resort owner. Perhaps a property offers rates that are so attractive that they cannot be passed up. But if the question of which property is most suitable is still undecided, the meeting planner must systematically evaluate potential properties until the best property emerges. In the same way that the size, timing, and cost of the meeting, organizational traditions and preferences, transportation and accessibility, and other considerations influenced site selection, so will some of these factors influence property selection.

Major Considerations

When there is no particular property in mind, there are three factors that primarily control property selection: 1) size, 2) cost, and 3) location. At all times, the participant profile must be kept in mind.

Whether size, cost, or location is more important varies depending on the meeting's characteristics. Obviously, for a small meeting, the planner has more choices because there are many more properties that can host 20 people than there are that can host 200. Cost may or may not matter to individual attendees. For example, if sales representatives have been invited to attend an incentive meeting, they do not pay their own costs, so it is management's meeting budget that counts. Cost and location are often intertwined, however; properties that are away from the mainstream are often less expensive. If several properties are suitable from the standpoints of size, cost, and location, then other, more subtle judgment calls must be made.

A meeting planner should ask direct questions about the renovation or building plans of a property that is under consideration as a meeting site. If extensive remodeling or construction are planned, great care should be made in booking a meeting. Nothing is more disturbing than the noise and confusion of construction. Most meeting planners will not schedule a meeting at a property if there is the slightest chance that a renovation will be in progress.

A meeting planner should also ask direct questions about what other groups are scheduled to use the property at the date of the meeting. Certain groups do not mingle well. A group that is seeking a retreat-like atmosphere, for example, might be distracted by a boisterous group of pleasure travelers. Although a property will naturally want to accommodate both groups if possible, the meeting planner should explain the meeting's objectives and the general characteristics of its participants to the property's sales representative.

Another factor that a meeting planner should consider is how courteously and consistently the property's sales staff responds to inquiries. If you have been negotiating with a property for four months and have been referred to three different sales representatives, it may reflect some instability among the property staff or indicate that your organization will not receive the level of service required for a successful meeting.

Size

The size of a property can immediately rule it in or out as a meeting site. If the property does not have the number of meeting rooms, guest rooms, and exhibit space that you need, then it is eliminated from consideration. If you need a hall that seats 300 and the property you are considering has an auditorium that only seats 250, it is not possible to use that property.

Most Convention and Visitors Bureaus distribute information about local accommodations that give information on the number of sleeping rooms, meeting and dining facilities, and exhibit spaces. This information usually includes dimensions and diagrams of meeting rooms.

Many reference books are also available that give this kind of information. The *Official Airline Guide Hotel/Motel Redbook Travel Planners*, the *Official Hotel and Resorts Guide*, and the *Hotel and Travel Index* are but a few resources.

Exhibit Space Requirements

Lack of exhibit space will quickly eliminate certain properties. If an exhibition or a trade show is an integral part of a meeting, then a property without adequate square footage cannot be considered. Many properties have adequate guest and meeting rooms for the majority of meetings but lack exhibit space. In some cases, however, the exhibition can be held at a location other than where the meeting participants will be lodged and fed.

Many conventions rely on the income from exhibits to offset administrative costs or at least the costs of the meeting. For this reason, many groups want to sell increasingly large amounts of exhibit space at their meetings. If an exhibit is important to the meeting, those properties unable to accommodate it can be quickly eliminated.

Function Room Requirements

The number and size of meeting rooms is considered next. Some prefer to call these meeting rooms *function rooms*. The term refers to rooms that are used for meeting sessions and meals. To estimate a meeting's function room needs, look at the dummy program and count the number of sessions and the number of participants expected at each one. Remember that if you have special setup needs, there must be time for the property staff to wheel in or take down equipment, rearrange tables and chairs, and so on.

Most meetings have at least one general session where all attendees are brought together. Some programs consist exclusively of general sessions. Usually, a property that wants to be competitive in the meeting business will have a room that will accommodate at least as many people as its total number of rooms. For example, if there are 400 rooms, then the ballroom will accommodate 400 guests. A meeting planner should be wary of contracting with a property that promises to find room for everyone despite evidence that it is short of what is needed in terms of the number and size of function rooms.

The following example illustrates how to estimate your meeting room requirements. Your meeting may begin with a general session at 9:00 A.M. Then, at 10:30 A.M., the group will break into three smaller group. Lunch will be held for the whole group at noon. Afternoon breakout sessions will begin at 2:00 P.M.

Thus, the function rooms needs for the day are a large room for two sessions, three smaller rooms before lunch, and three in the afternoon. Unless a reception were planned for that evening, the large room would not be needed again that day.

Guest Room Requirements

Without an accurate count of how many people will attend the meeting, the number of guest rooms has to be estimated primarily through meeting history. If 150 people attended a meeting last year, then 150 will probably be the minimum number to expect this year, unless last year's meeting was dismal. If an organization's membership has increased dramatically or if a business has greatly expanded its work force, then the expected attendance figure must be increased. Attendance at meetings grew 80 percent a year between 1983 and 1989.

Looking at the participant profile gives an idea as to the number of double or single rooms needed. Will attendees be rooming with each other? For some family-oriented organizations, children may be housed in the rooms with their parents. The meeting planner also has to estimate the number of participants that will arrive early, leave early, or stay after the meeting is over, because these factors will affect the guest room count.

Remember also that staff members may arrive early to prepare for the meeting. Often these people also stay an extra day or two to close down the details and pack up supplies used at the meeting, sometimes just to rest. A meeting property has to be able to accommodate these extra nights. When booking a meeting, the planner establishes ''block'' dates, usually including the two days prior and after the meeting. The property offers the convention room rate for these additional days.

Sleeping rooms are priced according to the number of persons using them and their location within the property. For example, poolside rooms usually cost more. Double rooms cost more than single rooms. Rooms that are considered deluxe because of amenities such as jaccuzis or wet bars cost more than more modest rooms. Some people do not mind sharing rooms, but the majority of meeting attendees do not want to be roomed with someone. People who are responsible for presentations at the meeting or employees who travel frequently may be especially picky about this. For most meetings, the safest bet is to assume that all attendees will want a single room.

Most properties classify their guest rooms in the following categories:

❑ **Single room**—Accommodates one person, usually in a double, queen, or king-sized bed.
❑ **Double room**—Accommodates two people in a double or queen or king-sized bed.
❑ **Twin double**—Accommodates two people in two twin, double, queen, or king-sized beds.
❑ **Double–double**—Accommodates two to four people in two double or queen-sized beds.
❑ **Triple**—Accommodates three people in a number of bed sizes (perhaps three twin beds or a double bed and a twin bed).
❑ **Quad**—Accommodates four people in two to four beds.
❑ **Suite**—Accommodates one or more people; includes a living room and one or two bedrooms with various numbers and sizes of beds.

Merely knowing that a property has 250 double rooms and 150 singles does not mean that 400 rooms are available for your organization's meeting. Other conventions may be also booked for the dates of your meeting. Hotels may have arrangements with corporations that guarantee space, so that there is never a time that the entire property is available.

The number of suites available at the property may be a factor. For example, a stockholders' annual meeting may involve 100 people, 20 of whom are on the corporate board of directors. If one board member is given suite accommodations, most likely the others will expect that. Thus, the property has to have 20 suites that are of equal or similar size and luxury.

Another consideration is whether the property has nonsmoking guest rooms. It is estimated that it takes $200 to eliminate the residue that smoke leaves on carpets, drapes, bed linens, and other furnishings from the typical room.

If the size of a property is satisfactory, cost and location are then appraised.

Cost

Most people would truly enjoy a meeting at the Greenbriar in White Sulphur Springs, West Virginia, The Cloisters in Sea Island, Georgia, or the

Hotel del Coronado in San Diego, but the vast majority of meeting participants cannot afford these five-star properties. On the other hand, some meetings demand luxury and the meeting sponsors or attendees will not look askance at the five-star price that comes with them.

The participant profile will eliminate certain properties as meeting choices on the basis of cost. For the average meeting planner, a knowledge of a property's "rack rate" (the standard price of a sleeping room, or the price that is offered the public) shows which properties are realistically within the attendees' budgets. Rack rates are those that are generally quoted in reference books and sales brochures. Group rates and off-season rates will be lower.

Location

After assessing properties for size and cost, the meeting planner considers location. In general, the choices are: 1) center cities; 2) suburbs; 3) airports; 4) resorts; and 5) alternative lodgings.

The participant profile helps the meeting planner know what atmosphere the meeting audience prefers.

Center Cities

Holding a meeting in the heart of a metropolitan area has both advantages and disadvantages. For large meetings that involve multiple properties, numerous guest rooms are usually available within short distances in a downtown location.

Moreover, properties that cater to the meeting business have traditionally been located in center city locations. Convention centers are most often located downtown.

Another advantage of center city locations is that usually a large number of restaurants and shops are within walking distance of hotels. Transportation, both from the airport and during the meeting, is easily accessible for downtown meeting locations. Taxis, public buses, and subway systems are available.

However, many travelers are deterred by the perception that there is more crime in the downtown areas of some metropolitan cities. Because of the general suburbanization of the American populace, many downtown areas are empty. Also, downtown areas typically do not have the recreational facilities that are available at other locations. Another disadvantage is the lack of parking and its high price in downtown areas.

Suburbs

Many fine meeting properties have been built in the suburbs of larger cities. These are often located within the proximity of large shopping centers or malls. This presents a variety of shops and restaurants for meeting attendees to enjoy. Parking is usually abundant.

Suburban properties are usually newer, and many are quite elegant.

Often they have recreational facilities of their own or are accessible to golf, tennis, and swimming facilities.

Some suburban areas have a disadvantage because they are located some distance from airports, bus terminals, or train stations. Transportation during the meeting may be a bit more difficult to arrange, but many suburbs have ever-improving public transportation.

Airports

Airport properties have seen tremendous growth (see Figure 6.1). More medium-sized convention centers are being built close to airports, thereby reducing the time that attendees spend traveling. Most airport properties have regular shuttle bus services between the airport and their facilities.

Many airport properties are newer, with modern meeting facilities. Often airports themselves rent office space daily or hourly, offering secretarial services, fax machines, computers, copying machines, and other business needs.

A disadvantage of airport lodging facilities is that they tend to be noisy. The lack of quality restaurants, shopping, and recreational facilities may also be a negative factor in choosing an airport property as a meeting site.

Resorts

There are resort *areas*, such as Aspen, Colorado, and Hilton Head, South Carolina, and there are resort *properties* at resort areas. The term *resort* can refer to either a place or a specific property. The primary advantages of resorts are usually recreational facilities and excellent service.

If a resort area such as Nassau, The Bahamas, or Snowshoe, Utah, is chosen, then the meeting planner decides exactly which property to book. Most properties in resort areas offer the same recreational facilities and comparable prices, so the decision of which property to use may be based on less concrete factors such as efficiency of service and the friendliness of the staff.

Some resorts are more geared to the pleasure traveler, not the business traveler. Such a relaxed atmosphere might not be attuned to the objectives of your meeting. On the other hand, resorts are excellent choices for incentive meetings that are rewards for good performance.

City	Number of Airport Motels	Total Number of Rooms
Atlanta	24	5,400
O'Hare (Chicago)	27	4,800
Los Angeles	53	13,116
Houston	34	8,400

Source: Copyright © 1990 by CMP Publications, Inc., 600 Community Drive, Mannhasset, NY 11030. Reprinted from Business Travel NEWS with permission.

Figure 6.1 **Accommodations Near Major Airports**

Alternative Properties

Campgrounds, campuses, cruise ships, and conference centers are four kinds of alternative properties. Campgrounds are suitable for certain group meetings such as church retreats. Other groups such as medical researchers may desire a campus setting, which offers classroom laboratories and a general aura of academia. Cruise ships are becoming more popular as meeting sites, particularly for incentive trips.

Conference centers are the newest alternative for meetings. These may be located in the center city, in the suburbs, or at airports. Conference centers are properties that cater exclusively to meetings. Often, meeting rooms are equipped with computers and lend themselves to sophisticated instructional needs. The government and some corporations have built their own conference centers, which are available for rent. The need for a conference center might narrow the meeting planner's property options.

Efficiency and Service

The factors discussed so far can be measured. If all of them are equal, the property's level of efficiency an service become evaluation factors. They cannot be as easily measured, but they can certainly be assessed.

Efficiency is defined as acting effectively with a minimum of waste and time, and the level of efficiency that you can observe when you contact or visit a property gives a clue as to how smoothly your meeting will go. On a site inspection, as you check in, evaluate the registration card and payment requirements. Observe the amount of paper shuffling. Is there a line of people waiting to register? Is your luggage handled efficiently?

Great service can make a meeting an unparalleled success. The more luxurious the property, the more likely you are to receive excellent service.

Basic to service is communication. Property staff and management must have open lines of communication with meeting planning staff and meeting attendees. The meeting planner should expect prompt, clear, and obliging communications with the sales and catering departments when booking the meeting. The meeting planner should be introduced to the property's general manager, catering director, reservations director, front desk manager, and housekeeping director. A convention services manager (CSM) should be assigned to the meeting planner during the meeting.

During the site inspection, try to observe a meeting in progress. Note if walkie-talkies or a registration desk telephone is used by the staff or between meeting planners and their CSMs.

The attitude of the property staff can be a deciding factor in choosing a particular property. Friendliness and courtesy are basic. See if staff go beyond the call of duty. You should assume that the staff knows when a meeting planner is on an evaluation visit and that they will try to do their best.

Luxury services to note are whether breakfast and newspapers are delivered to the guest rooms, whether cable television is available, whether beds are turned down, and whether there is a valet or bell service. A concierge is the ultimate luxury. These luxury services improve the ambience of a meeting. The presence of restaurants, coffee shops, gift stores, hairdressers, and florists on the property also benefit the meeting attendees. A property may offer additional personal care services, such as dry cleaning pick up and delivery, steam rooms, irons and ironing boards, and even masseuses!

Offering computers, FAX, copiers, and secretarial services is certainly a plus for a property. Sometimes this service is offered to the meeting planner only, or it may be offered to all guests.

Successful Meetings magazine annually names its Pinnacle Award winners—those properties judged by meeting planners as the best meeting properties.

EFFICIENCY AND SERVICE CHECKLIST

Rate each of the following on a 1–5 scale as follows: Excellent = 5, Good = 4, Average = 3, Below Average = 2, Poor = 1.

Score   Characteristic

_____   The sales department has communicated promptly and courteously.

_____   The site inspection included introductions to management and staff.

_____   Property staff were efficient and friendly during the check-in process.

_____   Bell service personnel are helpful.

_____   Other uniformed staff are efficient and friendly.

_____   The housekeeping staff is efficient and friendly.

The quality of the food services in the following facilities was at the level desired:

_____   Restaurant

_____   Bars

_____   Room Service

The quality of recreational facilities was at the level desired.

_____   Pool

_____   Sauna

_____   Tennis/Golf

_____   Exercise Room

_____   Other

_____   There are shops or stores on the property with a suitable variety and quality of merchandise.

_____   There is office support.

_____   The transportation service is adequate.

_____   **Total Score**

Inspecting the Property

So far, the size, cost range, and location of several properties may be suitable. What is the next step in the decision-making process?

Making on-site inspection visits is the best method of confirming the choice of a meeting site. Actually see—and try out—the different contenders. Although it might be best for the meeting planner to visit incognito as an average business traveler, most budgets don't allow this. Properties will usually give complimentary rooms to meeting planners on inspection tours. Convention and Visitors Bureaus and Chambers of Commerce join in welcoming meeting planners and trying to influence a possible meeting decision. Wining and dining are the name of the game if the meeting is of sufficient size or distinction.

Checklists enable one to equally measure one property against another. The lists include concrete requirements and intangible subtleties. These lists should be customized for each different meeting.

General Evaluation

The general evaluation of a property includes space and cost factors. But questions should be asked and observations made on a variety of other factors as well.

Ask about the security of the property. Will your attendees feel safe inside the property and on its grounds? How secure will registration material be if left overnight at the meeting registration desk?

Observe notices about fire exits. Are they numerous and visible? Are there fire extinguishers or sprinkler systems throughout the property? Ask about emergency procedures established for fires or individual health problems. Staff knowledge of CPR, the nearness of hospital emergency rooms and fire departments, and other such factors could save a life in an emergency.

Ask the sales representative what level of liability insurance the property carries. Adequate property damage insurance is especially important if the meeting includes an exhibit. Some meeting planners contract for floater policies for specific meetings.

GENERAL PROPERTY CHECKLIST

Rate each of the following on a 1–5 scale as follows: Excellent = 5, Good = 4, Average = 3, Below Average = 2, Poor = 1.

Score   Characteristic

_____ The property is willing to block an adequate number of guest rooms.

_____ An adequate number of suites are available.

_____ The property is willing to block dates.

_____ The block price is reasonable.

_____ Cancellation fees are reasonable.

_____ There is check-in and check-out time flexibility

_____ There is an adequate number of suitable function rooms available.

_____ There is adequate space for exhibits.

_____ No other distracting meetings are booked at same time.

_____ Location from airport (describe) _____

_____ Airport transfers are convenient.

_____ Transportation is available.

_____ The level of luxury expected is evident.

_____ There is good accessibility for handicapped persons.

_____ Security is adequate.

_____ Emergency preparedness is evident.

_____ Food service is available and of good quality.

_____ Recreation is available (list) _____

_____ Entertainment is available (list) _____

_____ Storage is available.

_____ There are adequate facilities for bringing in freight.

_____ Registration cards are available.

_____ Directional signs are available.

_____ **Total Score**

Guest Rooms

On a site inspection, the meeting planner should inspect each type of guest room that is offered—double room, single room, and so forth—and should look at several of them. Visit rooms on several different floors and rooms with different views, such as street side, poolside, and rear side.

GUEST ROOM CHECKLIST

Rate each of the following on a 1–5 scale as follows: Excellent = 5, Good = 4, Average = 3, Below Average = 2, Poor = 1.

Score   Characteristic

_____   The rooms are clean (dusted, vacuumed, bath scrubbed, carpet clean, windows and mirrors polished, linens spotless).

_____   The rooms are in good repair (carpet/bedspread/drapes not frayed, caulking in bath not chipping, window/doors/drapes operating).

_____   The decor is attractive.

_____   There is adequate lighting.

_____   There is adequate security.

_____   There is good ventilation.

_____   The heating and air conditioning systems and controls are operating.

_____   There is a telephone (list if no charge for room-to-room service, charge for local calls) _____

_____

_____   The rooms' location and views are generally satisfactory.

_____   Extras are provided (for refrigerator, coffee maker, free HBO, closed channel TV, bill review, bed turn down service, give 2 points each).

_____   Samples of toiletries, large towels, etc. are provided (give 1 point each)

_____   **Total Score**

Function Rooms

Where the meeting rooms are located and their proximity to each other is important. Ideally, all rooms used will be on the same floor so that attendees do not have to use elevators. Even large properties with several dozen elevators never seem to be able to handle the crowds when several meetings adjourn at the same time.

The comfort of the meeting room—its chairs, ventilation, and lighting—is important. An unobstructed view of the speaker's podium or stage is vital. The acoustics of the room should be checked. At certain meetings, confidential material is discussed. If so, dividers and walls should be reasonably soundproofed. Having the proper audiovisual equipment and enough outlets is important. Chapter 10 gives more details on function rooms.

FUNCTION ROOM CHECKLIST

Rate each of the following on a 1–5 scale as follows: Excellent = 5, Good = 4, Average = 3, Below Average = 2, Poor = 1.

Score   **Characteristic**

_____   The rooms are suitably located to:

    _____   Other meeting rooms

    _____   Elevators and escalators

    _____   Restrooms

    _____   Food service

    _____   Phones

_____   The decor is attractive.

_____   Chairs are comfortable.

_____   The podium view is unobscured.

_____   The room is soundproofed and its acoustics are good.

_____   Fire regulations are posted.

_____   There is good ventilation.

_____   There is good lighting.

_____   There are enough electrical outlets.

_____   A stage is available.

_____   There is adequate A/V equipment and hook-ups:

    _____   Microphones

    _____   VCRs

    _____   Film/slide projectors

    _____   Permanent screens

    _____   Podiums, easels, and chalkboards

_____   There are table coverings.

_____   Extras are provided (pencils, pads, etc.) (give 1 point each).

_____   The function room costs are reasonable (list) _____

_____   Total Score

Exhibit Space

As stated previously, trade show/exhibition management is complicated. Thus, only the basic requirements of small- to medium-sized exhibits that accompany a meeting are covered in the sample checklist that follows.

EXHIBIT SPACE CHECKLIST

Rate each of the following on a 1–5 scale as follows: Excellent = 5, Good = 4, Average = 3, Below Average = 2, Poor = 1.

Score   Characteristic

_____   The exhibit space is well located with respect to function rooms.

_____   Booth placements are suitable for this type of exhibit.

_____   There are unobstructed pathways.

_____   There is adequate electrical service.

_____   Tables and separating curtains are available.

_____   Contractors are available (if needed).

_____   Labor unions are cooperative.

_____   There is adequate security.

_____   There is good lighting.

_____   There is good ventilation.

_____   **Total Score**

Food Service

The planner should eat in the restaurants on the property. Some hotels may have two or three restaurants that vary in terms of formality and cost. Look at the menu variety and the service and quality of the food. If there are meetings in progress during the meeting planner's visit, the catering staff should be observed. The path used to transport food to function rooms should be traced. The planner will be shown catering menus with food prices and can evaluate if they meet the meeting's needs.

Negotiating the Cost

Do you know how to bargain? How to haggle with a merchant to get a lower price? Skilled negotiators make good meeting planners.

There are three major costs involved at meeting sites. These are the costs for sleeping rooms, function rooms, and meals. For groups, a property's standard or rack rates should be lowered. As noted, a large number of meeting participants or the time of year at which the meeting is held can be factors that may lower the room price. A property may be willing to lower its rates for a prestigious meeting. Property managers will offer the better price because they anticipate favorable publicity if famous people stay at their facilities.

Some properties quote a government rate or corporate rate to meeting planners. The corporate rate is usually negotiated between a property and a company. The company knows that it will use a certain number of rooms each month and guarantees this to receive a lower price. For example, airlines contract with airport properties to accommodate flight personnel who have frequent layovers. Knowing the corporate rate is helpful to the meeting planner. As mentioned in Chapter 5, government agencies must work within established per diems. A property that anticipates that a large number of government employees will need lodging throughout the year will offer a government rate that meets the per diem.

Certain properties that are part of a chain have frequent user programs. If a person stays in one of the chain's properties for five nights, then she or he receives a discount for a sixth night. Knowing this discounted rate is helpful to the meeting planner in negotiating sleeping room price.

Most properties quote rates for single rooms, double rooms, rooms with extra persons, and suites. Occasionally, the single and double room rates are the same, or the rate is the same no matter where the room is located within the property.

A property will block or reserve a certain number of rooms at an agreed-upon price. Dates that the price is effective should include the two days prior to the opening and two days after closing the meeting. At some point, usually three weeks prior to the meeting, the reservation is released and the room price reverts to the rack rate. The date at which the room commitment is released can be negotiated.

When meetings are planned years in advance, a room rate can be negotiated with a clause specifying a maximum percentage that the rate can rise. For example, a $90 rate may be agreed upon now, but the meeting is not scheduled until 1996. Of course, prices will rise during that time, but the contract will state specifically that the room rate can only increase by five percent.

Discuss check-in and check-out times. Set cancellation fees and refunds. Get information on how to establish credit with the property. Discuss how the Master Account, which reflects all charges such as food and beverage costs that the meeting organization will pay directly, will be set up and reconciled. Request to review it daily. If the organization is paying the room charges for speakers, presenters, and staff, clarify which charges will be paid by the organization and which will be the responsibility of individuals.

Several charges depend on the number of room nights booked. Room nights equal the number of participants staying at the property multiplied by the number of nights they stay. If 150 attendees stay at a property for three nights, 450 room nights are booked.

Whether complimentary sleeping rooms and suites are offered is based on the number of room nights. Commonly, one complimentary room night is offered for every fifty room nights booked. Usually, to have a complimentary suite for one night, one would need to 100 room nights.

Function	
From	Motorinn Plaza 123 Main Street Anytown, USA
Contact	J. Wren 234 First Street Everytown, USA
Conference Dates	Thurs., Oct. 6–Sat., Oct. 8, 19__.
Rate Dates	Tues, Oct. 4–Mon., OCt. 10, 19__.
Guest Room Commitment	500 room nights
Guest Room Rates	Single: $90 1 Bdrm. Suite: $170 Double: $110 2 Bdrm. Suite: $200 For your event, the following rates will be in effect: Single: $75 1 Bdrm. Suite: $150 Double: $90 2 Bdrm. Suite: $175 (Net rates. Non-commissionable.) All rates are subject to state tax, which is 5%, and the city hotel tax of 5%.
Estimated Occupancy	Single, 80%; double 20%

Arrival Pattern

Arrivals		*In-House*
Tues., Oct. 4	5	5
Wed., Oct. 5	150	155
Thurs. Oct. 6	20	175
Fri., Oct. 7	5	180

Departures		*In-House*
Fri., Oct. 7	15	165
Sat., Oct. 8	50	115
Sun., Oct. 9	110	5

(Check-in time is 2:00 P.M. daily. Unguaranteed reservations are released at 5:00 P.M. Check-out time is 12 noon.)

Cut-Off Time	Three (3) weeks prior to your major arrival date, Wednesday, Oct. 5, 19__, which is Sept. 15, 19__, the remaining portion of your guest room commitment will be released, but the Motorinn Plaza will continue to accept reservations on the basis of availability at the prevailing range of published Motorinn Plaza prices.

Figure 6.2 Sample Property Contract

Reservations	Your organization will be supplied, at no charge, a reasonable number of reservation cards that explain the room rate reduction and cut-off date.
Complimentary Guest Rooms	The Motorinn Plaza will confirm a complimentary guest room ration of one (1) room night for every fifty (50) room nights actually utilized over the main dates of your event. You may elect to apply some of individual units to suites at one (1) room night for every one hundred (100) room nights utilized.
	The assignment of your complimentary accommodations will be made by your office and apply only over the dates of your scheduled program. Complimentary rooms must be utilized and cannot be credited to your Master Account.
Public Space	Following is an outline of the meeting program and the public space reserved as we now understand it. We reserve the right to substitute meeting space, provided it is suitable to your needs.

Day/Date/Function	Time	Room	Attendance
Thursday, Oct. 6			
General Session	9:00–10:00	Ballroom	300
Two Breakout Rooms	10:00–12:00	Admiral/Captain	100/200
Lunch	12:00–2:00	Ballroom	275
Two Breakout Rooms	2:00–5:00	Admiral/Captain	150/150
Friday, Oct. 7			
Breakfast	8:00–9:30	Ballroom	275
Three Breakout Rooms	9:30–12:30	Admiral/Captain/ Commander	100 each
Lunch	12:30–2:00	On Own	
Two Breakout Rooms	2:00–5:00	Admiral/Captain	150/150
Reception	6:00–8:00	Trident	275
Banquet	8:00–10:30	Ballroom	250
Saturday, Oct. 8			
Breakfast	8:00–9:00	Admiral/Captain	200
General Session	9:00–10:30	Ballroom	200
Sponsored Coffee Break	10:30–11:30	Admiral/Captain	175

Space will be made available for a registration desk in the vicinity of the ballroom. Ten (10) exhibit tables will be set up in the Atrium. Coffee will be available in the

(continued)

Figure 6.2 (continued)

	Atrium from 10:30–11:30 A.M. and 3:30–4:30 P.M. on Thursday, Oct. 6, and Friday, October 7, 19___.
Meeting Arrangements	A Convention Services Manager will be in contact with you 90 days prior to the event to arrange meeting room, audiovisual, and food and beverage requirements.
Public Space Cost	In consideration of the food and beverage activities and the attendance indicated, as well as the guest room commitment the following rental for the meeting rooms is in effect:

Total Room Nights Used 10/6–10/8, 19___	Total Meeting Room Rental
0–99	$15,000
100–299	$12,000
300–499	$ 8,000
700–Above	Complimentary

Payment	All participants will pay for room, tax, and incidental charges on an individual basis. Policy requires full prepayment for all services unless credit and master billing arrangements are established in advance. If desired, please request our credit application. If approved, a Master Account will be prepared for all banquet, rental, and exhibit charges plus any specified incidental charges outlined by you.
Arbitration	Any controversy or claim arising out of or relating to the cancellation of this contract shall be settled in accordance with the Rules of the American Arbitration Association and judgment upon the award rendered by the Arbitrator(s) may be entered in any court.
Cancellation	The following represents a reasonable effort on behalf of the hotel to establish its actual damages for cancellation and such schedule shall represent Liquidated Damages for cancellation of this agreement.
	Cancellation of agreement within thirty (30) days of event date: $10,000 penalty; 31–60 days: $7,500 penalty; 61–90 days: $5,000 penalty, payable to the Motorinn Plaza.

If these arrangements meet with your approval, please sign and return and the agreement shall become binding.

_____   _____
Prepared by   Event Coordinator

Figure 6.2 (continued)

Function room rates also depend on room nights. A ballroom might cost $16,000 for a three-day meeting. When the meeting sponsor books 300 room nights, the rate might be lowered to $6,000. If 600 room nights are booked, there may be no charge for the ballroom. Function room rates may also be lowered or waived if the meeting contracts for a certain number of meals to be provided to attendees. Food and beverage costs depend on menus, and their prices are not usually written into the property contract.

Keep in mind the high sales taxes and hotel/visitor taxes that are imposed in some cities and counties. Nonprofit organizations do not have to pay these and their price negotiations should note this.

Figure 6.2 shows a sample property contract.

CHAPTER ACTIVITIES

Complete the sample checklists by visiting two properties in your area. Call ahead to talk with the sales department and explain your project.

Marketing Your Meeting

Upon completion of this chapter, you will be able to:

1. Decide what factors will influence attendance at a particular meeting

2. Judge which method(s) of marketing best suit a particular meeting

3. Develop printed materials

4. Estimate what it will cost to market the meeting

T he nightmarish vision includes an empty mailbox, gallons of tepid coffee, unused nametags, empty chairs, and the hollow sound in an almost-empty room. It takes people to meet, and a meeting planner's fear is having no participants or fewer participants than expected.

Marketing combines the four Ps: Product, Place, Price, and Promotion. The product is the meeting, the place is the meeting site, and the price is determined. Now promotion must be the concentration.

Marketing denotes selling. Does one have to sell a meeting? In some instances, the meeting has such appeal that participants swamp the meeting sponsor or meeting planner with pleas to attend.

On the other hand, thousands of meetings are held daily. One person often belongs to several associations or common interest groups and is invited to numerous meetings each year. In addition, that person may have job-related business meetings to attend. In these instances, the meeting definitely has to be sold to participants.

For many people, the meeting supermarket is overstocked. Sophisticated marketing techniques must be used to get their attention (and then their participation). Today meetings must have a purpose, even though it may only be pleasure. This purpose must be clearly stated to prospective participants.

Chapter 3 included a discussion of how meeting planners estimate meeting attendance. Many decisions concerning the meeting and its associated costs are made in light of this number. From the standpoint of achieving attendance expectations, then, marketing the meeting takes on great significance. An excellent marketing effort can greatly increase the number of attendees at a meeting.

Why Market the Meeting?

Is "the more the merrier" always the case? Not always, but sometimes. Marketing meetings has three main purposes: 1) to notify everyone who is eligible to attend; 2) to increase attendance; and 3) to make money.

A great deal of marketing is simply a function of distributing information about when, where, and how to register to attend the meeting. A person who is qualified to attend and desirable as a meeting attendee may feel slighted if he or she never hears about the meeting.

When the number of participants at the meeting is below expectations, it diminishes the sense that the meeting was successful. If an organization's annual convention attracted 200 people last year and only 125 attend this year, obviously something has gone wrong. The meeting planner should be familiar with the organization's records of attendance and have clear aims and goals as to the attendance figures expected at a future meeting.

Certain organizations depend on the income from their meetings to fund their activities. To this end, a trade show, held in conjunction with a meeting, usually makes a profit. Charging admissions or selling meeting materials produces income.

When fund raising is a major reason for holding a meeting, marketing takes on even more importance. The meeting planner is under pressure to assure that attendance will generate the amount of income expected.

Knowing Your Audience

Whom do you want to come to your meeting? By defining your audience, you know to whom your marketing efforts should be directed.

Businesses and Associations

Many business meetings, held for a single company or corporation, are so-called command performances; thus, the marketing efforts need not be extensive. Corporate management holds the meeting and decides who is expected to attend. Those who are expected to attend have little choice in the matter. Marketing consists of merely notifying them about the meeting, yet the objectives and content of the meeting must still be clearly explained.

Most association meetings are optional. Members attend voluntarily, but they have to be convinced. Therefore, marketing to members must be persuasive and elaborate.

An association might be trying to increase its membership. Here the marketing effort is expanded to nonmembers—perhaps to some portion of the general public that has been identified as having interests in common with members of the association.

Finally, the attendance at some organizational meetings is limited to a few persons, such as a board of directors or a senior management team. Marketing to these smaller groups is nominal. The group is notified of the meeting and is expected to attend. For example, board members know that when they accept their board positions, they will have to attend meetings in order to carry on the business of their organization.

Consumers

Marketing for trade shows or seminars that are open to the public is an entirely different matter. These events are held for profit and anyone and everyone is invited. Newspaper advertising, television spots, and extensive direct mail efforts are aimed at getting people to attend the event.

Generally speaking, the sponsors of consumer trade shows and seminars have advertising and marketing professionals on staff. Sometimes a local marketing organization is hired to advertise the show or seminar.

What Sells a Meeting?

As mentioned, the decision of whether to attend a meeting is sometimes out of the hands of the prospective attendee, and marketing only involves notifying the person of where to be and when.

Most often, though, whether to attend a meeting is a personal decision. The features and benefits of attending must be outlined for and sold to the prospective participant. In doing so, the person who is marketing the meeting can emphasize the meeting's program content, external factors that might motivate a person to attend, or the ways in which the meeting can help the person to achieve personal goals or answer psychological needs.

Program Content

When someone decides to attend a meeting, usually it is because the meeting's objectives correspond with the person's needs. For example, the person might desire or be required to have further education and training. A person might also be motivated to attend a meeting because business or operational decisions about the organization will be made there. A sales representative who needs the equivalent of a pep talk might attend a meeting that introduces a new product. It becomes apparent, then, that the program content is most persuasive and that the meeting's marketing materials must do a good job of conveying program content.

Psychological and Personal Factors

There are psychological reasons that motivate a person to attend a meeting. Chief among them is prestige. Attending certain meetings gives one a feeling of success and status. Being part of a select group gives distinction. Wanting to be part of the "in crowd" influences attendance decisions.

The psychological theorist Abraham Maslow designed a hierarchy of human motivations. Attending a meeting satisfies psychological and self-actualization needs. The need for self-actualization motivates some people to learn. No matter what the actual objectives of the meeting or the session topics, the person gravitates toward any meeting that is perceived as presenting a learning environment.

A person might also be motivated to attend a meeting because of certain personal aims that have little to do with the reasons for or objective of the meeting. The meeting sessions are not going to answer these goals or desires. Opportunities to fulfill them are offered at the meeting but outside its structure.

Among these aims can be the wish to network among one's peers. Or someone might want to hold an elected office in an association; the person attends a meeting in order to get to know association members better and to be seen. Someone may want to change jobs and thus attends a meeting at which prospective employers can be found, perhaps a job fair or trade convention. Another person may be interested in talking with vendors at an exhibit to try to sell an invention. A strong motivation may be to mingle with friends and peers or to renew an acquaintance. Meetings provide an opportunity for these sorts of get-togethers, especially for people who do not live or work near each other.

At the same time that meeting marketing materials can emphasize the content of a meeting, they can also address the other factors that motivate a person to attend a meeting. These motivations can be appealed to subtly or openly. Marketing materials that highlight the opportunity to mingle with cohorts or insinuate that "everyone who is anyone will be there" answer some psychological motivations.

Other Factors

External factors also determine whether a person attends a meeting. Primary among these is location of the meeting and the individual's reaction to it. A longing to visit San Francisco might motivate a person to decide to attend a meeting there. Although a meeting may be program-intensive with little free time, the opportunity to visit a desirable location, possible tacking on extra vacation days, and perhaps even bringing the family may make the meeting irresistible.

Extracurricular or free-time activities that are planned for the meeting appeal to some people. For some, the side trips and local tours are the attraction. The opportunity to visit an exhibit or trade show can also be the sole reason for attending a meeting.

Marketing Methods

How does one spread the word about a meeting? There are many methods, including direct mail, advertising and publicity, promotional events, and telemarketing. Any single method can be used, or all methods can be combined in the marketing effort.

Of course, the marketing methods used must match the nature of the meeting, the projected size of the meeting, the characteristics of the participants, and the budget for the meeting. Timing—deciding when to advertise or send out direct mail—is also determined by the nature of the meeting and its participants. Some organizations will begin to market next year's annual convention at the close of this year's annual convention. Some business meetings may be called on two weeks' notice.

The primary method of promoting a meeting is through printed items such as letters, invitations, brochures, and flyers. The meeting might also be promoted with advertising and publicity in various publications.

Direct Mail

Direct mail is the mainstay of meeting marketing. Any number of promotional items such as letters, invitations, brochures, flyers, reservation forms, and giveaways can be delivered to the offices and homes of prospective meeting participants. Usually membership lists and company rosters supply the data for the mailing list. Mailing lists can be purchased and can be very specialized, listing people by residence, income level, and occupation.

❑ **Letters** provide the easiest means of notifying people that a meeting is being held. Computers can merge mailing lists, print out envelope labels, and personalize the letter's inside address and salutation. Although this is a straightforward marketing method, with today's masses of direct mail, a letter does not attract much attention.

Consider printing stationery specifically for the meeting that prominently displays the name, theme, and dates of the event. A stick-on label with this information can be designed to be placed on existing organization letterhead.

Letters can merely announce the meeting and give basic information about dates, location, and cost, or they can sell the meeting by telling people the features and benefits of attending the meeting. Figure 7.1 gives two examples of letters announcing a meeting.

❑ **Invitations** are a graceful alternative to letters. An invitation can be a distinct printed item. It can be engraved and formal, such as a wedding invitation, or it can be casual and friendly with hand-written copy and cartoon character art. The type of meeting and who is expected to attend indicates the degree of formality required.

Dear _____ :

The Association of Pipe Fitters announces its 23rd annual conference to be held in San Francisco, May 21–24, 19___ . The meeting will be held at the Sheraton Center Town. Enclosed please find a reservation card to be completed by you and returned directly to the hotel.

Dear _____ :

Learn the newest technology in your field. Create security for your employees. View over 75 exhibits of the latest installation equipment. Yes, the Association of Pipe Fitters 23rd annual conference is about to be a happening!

Find you heart in unforgettable San Francisco, May 21–24, 19___ . Offering the best in accommodations and magnificent food service, the Sheraton Center Town is the site for this exciting meeting.

Don't be left out! Send the postage-paid return reservation card today. We'll see you there!

Figure 7.1 **Sample Letters Announcing a Meeting**

A specific person can invite people to participate in the meeting. The person might be a well-known expert in the subject of the meeting, a renowned keynote speaker, or a celebrity. Mayors are often willing to invite conventioneers to their cities, and governors are usually happy to invite tourists and trade delegations.

❑ **Brochures** that give all the important information about the meeting are basic to meeting marketing. Brochures should include an outline of the program, brief biographies of noted speakers, opening and closing times, registration information, and information about the meeting property and transportation arrangements.

Brochures can be multi-page documents with four-color printing, or they can be quite simple. A brochure can include a registration card for the meeting.

The appeal of a geographical site should be capitalized on by including destination materials, with the mailed invitation or announcement. Certainly, state tourism offices, CVBs, and Chambers of Commerce are more than willing to give the meeting planner brochures that tout the city's tourist attractions.

❑ **Flyers** are single printed or copied pages that can be designed as self-mailers to be folded and sent to potential participants with no envelope costs. Since flyers are inexpensive to produce, they can also be used as inserts in routine mailings or sent in quantity to be placed where prospective participants might see them.

❑ **Reservation forms** for both the meeting and the hotel should be sent out as part of the marketing package. The meeting registration form, which actually serves as a reservation for the meeting, is an important marketing tool. For many meetings, this is the only printed marketing material used. Information about the registration form is discussed in Chapter 8.

Recipients of registration forms are instructed to return them to the meeting planner. The form itself can be a stamped (postage paid) postcard, a tear-off on a brochure or, most likely, a separate form to be returned in an envelope with registration payment.

Usually an organization will discount the registration fee if a person registers and pays by a certain date. This puts a bit of pressure on a person to go ahead and decide about attending. It also helps the meeting planner give more timely guarantees to the hotel for meals and arrangements.

The hotel usually provides its own reservation forms to be included in mailings; the forms are then mailed directly back to the property. The reservation department at the hotel processes these and tells the meeting planner how many have been received.

❑ **Sales promotion items,** sometimes called *giveaways*, can catch the attention of potential attendees. When the budget allows and when an all-out effort is to be made to increase meeting attendance, a huge variety of pens, pencils, caps, calendars, playing cards, key rings, and hundreds of other items can be ordered and mailed. These items advertise the name of the meeting sponsor and the meeting theme, dates, and location.

Giveaways can either tie into the theme, logo, or slogan that has been adopted for the meeting or they can convey the tone of the meeting. Simply putting confetti into an envelope with an invitation conveys "party time."

One chamber of commerce recently held a fund-raising ball and used a frisbee printed with the pertinent data about the event as the invitation. Though it was more costly than an engraved invitation, the frisbee certainly caught everyone's attention when it was hand-delivered to those on the invitation list.

As mentioned in Chapter 5, a city's CVB or DMO sometimes has promotional items to donate to organizations holding important meetings in its area. Newport, Rhode Island, might give away keychains shaped like sail boats; Seattle might use the Space Needle; a resort in upstate New York might use an Adirondack chair. For certain meetings, the DMO may purchase and contribute a giveaway as part of its promotional arrangements with the meeting organization.

Other giveaways might be donated by the hotel. Match packs, cocktail napkins, pens, stationery, and miniature copies of menus, all imprinted with the hotel name, are items that most hotels stock and are willing to give to the marketing effort. Sending one item with each marketing mailing is effective. Remember that both the property and the meeting city benefit by hosting meetings, so asking for this type of assistance is reasonable.

Figure 7.2 shows sample giveaways.

Advertising and Publicity

Newsletters, magazines, and newspapers are marketing vehicles. They carry meeting information in the form of paid advertising and in the form of free publicity.

When an organization wishes to advertise its meeting, the meeting planner determines desirable publications and investigates space costs, issue dates, deadlines, and art requirements. An ad can be designed simply as an announcement, using a variety of typefaces for its layout, or it can be a four-color creation planned by an advertising firm.

Publicity is free advertising. When a publication prints information on a meeting as a news story or feature article, interest (and most likely attendance) at the meeting are increased. Publicity is generated by sending news releases to various publications. The planner compiles a list of appropriate media that would be likely to print information about the meeting. A press release can announce the date and time of the meeting, name sponsors, highlight speakers, and summarize program content.

The organization sponsoring the meeting may publish its own newsletter or magazine. If the entire membership is invited to an organization's meeting, the meeting should be heavily publicized in the newsletter or magazine.

Figure 7.2 Sample Giveaways

Other organizations with missions or goals that are similar to the meeting sponsor's are usually happy to sell an ad or run an article on the meeting in their publications. When seeking to increase attendance at a meeting, brainstorming about who would be interested in the meeting can generate creative ideas about which publications to send press releases to or where to advertise. For example, the Jonquil Growers of America might welcome the Tulip Growers of America to attend their convention. In return, the Tulip Growers would be glad to announce the next Jonquil Growers conference. Similarly, pharmaceutical meetings could attract participants by placing ads in medical association magazines.

Business management magazines are usually amenable to advertising and editorializing about meetings that would be of interest to their readers. If the organization holding the meeting is nonprofit, there may be no charge for an ad.

Promotional Events

Marketing an upcoming meeting can occur during an ongoing meeting. For example, if next year's annual convention will be held in New Orleans, then a theme luncheon could be held at this year's meeting to announce it. Possibly the Chamber of Commerce would donate a giveaway, and surely brochures, for that luncheon. To literally whet attendees' appetite for New Orleans, the menu could feature Cajun or French food.

National organizations may rely on their local or regional offices or chapters to market general meetings. The national headquarters might send a speaker to the local area to promote attendance. Promotional materials might be sent to local organizations for distribution.

For consumer meetings, which by definition are open to the public, press conferences, announcement receptions, and ribbon-cuttings are common methods of marketing meetings. They attract publicity and photos, which in turn attract the public's attention and cultivate interest in the event.

The meeting planner coordinates, schedules, and stages these promotional events. The aim is to inform anyone who needs to know about future meetings and to promote attendance.

Telemarketing

A phone call can frequently convince a person to attend a meeting. Particularly if a person who is prominent in an organization has not sent in a meeting reservation, a phone call from someone is in order. When arranging national or regional meetings, phoning local offices or chapters is useful as a marketing tool and also to get an idea of the number of representatives that will attend from their locales.

These marketing calls may be made by officers, directors, paid staff, or at-large members of the organization. On the other hand, professional telemarketers may be hired to phone prospective participants. The planner must give them detailed scripts and training, particularly if phone reservations are being taken.

When an airline is working with the meeting planner and has offered a discounted ticket price, sometimes its reservations personnel will phone prospective attendees to encourage them to attend the meeting and offer to book their flight arrangements. It is less likely, but still possible, that sales representatives from a hotel or rental car agency will assist with telemarketing.

Designing Marketing Materials

All of a meeting's marketing materials should send a message to prospective meeting participants that the meeting is important and that the participants' attendance is desirable.

The design of promotional materials for a meeting should include a meeting logo. Logos are symbols that provide instant identification with a product or company. IBM, American Airlines, McDonald's, Sheraton, and Coca-Cola are examples of corporations that have universally familiar logos.

Many meetings adopt themes that then inspire a meeting logo. Some themes can be conveyed by a brief slogan. Familiar objects may inspire a meeting theme. For example, umbrellas, apples, blankets, door knockers, and pocket knives are a few items that suggest themes. They can also be used as giveaways to promote a meeting. For example, a keychain and key might suggest "Opening the Door to the Future." A fake $100 bill can symbolize "Increasing Profits."

A meeting logo should be an integral part of all meeting materials. Using the logo gives continuity to printed materials and provides an image for the organization.

In designing marketing materials, the planner should keep the following information in mind:

❏ **Typeface.** A variety of interesting typefaces is available for letters, invitations, brochures, and flyers. Thanks to desktop publishing and laser printers, camera-ready copy that is both clear enough and clean enough to be used for printing can be produced by many offices.

For promotional materials, choose an easy-to-read typeface in a size large enough for comfortable reading. Leave enough white space so that the printed material is not crowded.

Sample typefaces are shown in Figure 7.3.

❏ **Stock.** The grade of paper on which the marketing materials are printed suggests the meeting's degree of formality. If the registration fee for a two-day seminar is more than $500, people expect materials to be printed on something better than simple copier paper.

Paper is graded by weight. Heavier paper feels more elegant and expensive, which, of course, it is. Ink is less likely to bleed through heavier paper, which makes it more suitable for two-sided printing.

Paper sheen also conveys quality. Glossy paper, which is called *coated stock*, has a slight reflective shine that connotes sophistication and refinement. Coated stock is slightly more expensive.

Figure 7.3 **Sample Typefaces**

Paper textures, such as pebble or woven, also communicate quality. Though more expensive, sometimes a woven paper is exactly right for conveying a subtle message about the atmosphere and level of luxury that attends certain meetings.

❑ **Color.** Colors can connote a theme and atmosphere. Yellow suggests sun and gaiety. Red, white, and blue represent patriotism. Wine, navy blue, and beige suggest refinement. The colors of both the paper and the ink used in marketing materials should fit in with the meeting's theme or the type of organization.

Inks can be screened (made lighter) to give different effects. A bright red can be screened to a pale pink. Different colored papers show various colored inks to different degrees. They must complement each other.

The use of one color of ink does not add much to the cost of printing, nor does the use of colored paper. These inexpensive options can add an aura of class or a touch of fun to any meeting's promotional materials. Keep in mind that the use of four-color photographs is very expensive. The cost of making the separations and printing is extremely high. Few organizations or businesses have marketing budgets large enough to afford this.

For all printed materials, remember that from the time a rough sketch is made, bids are taken, and the piece is typeset, printed, folded, stuffed, metered, and mailed, several weeks have passed. It is best to begin preparing printed materials at last two months before the targeted mail date.

Marketing Costs

If the success of a meeting is measured to any extent by attendance figures, then marketing costs can become big items in the meeting budget. Fortunately, most marketing costs can be accurately estimated. Newspapers and magazines make their advertising rates available, and print costs can be estimated within a certain range. The costs for promotional events and telemarketing are not as simple to establish, because they often hinge on labor costs.

Since a good deal of the marketing effort will involve direct mail, the cost of postage must be figured. The planner should determine how many mailings are appropriate. A sample schedule might be:

How long before meeting	Item
5 months	Announcement
4 months	Formal invitation
3 months	Geographical site and hotel information
2 months	Reminder flyer

Here there would be four mailings. Keep in mind that the weight of what is being mailed will affect the cost of postage. For example a hotel brochure, a city map, and matchbook from the hotel will cost more to mail than the announcement flyer.

Great savings can be realized by using bulk mail instead of first-class postage. For bulk (or third-class) mailings, a certain amount of labor is involved because letters to each zip code must be sorted, banded, and labeled. Bulk mail houses will do all of this, of course, for a price. Nonprofit organizations get a break on postage costs and qualify for second-class mail rates, which are even more economical. Local post offices can advise organizations on mailing materials. They can tell organizations how many pieces of mail are needed to qualify for bulk mailing and provide information on organizing a bulk mailing.

To calculate the cost of mailing, multiply the number of pieces sent by the cost of postage. For example, if there are 1,000 members of an association, and flyers cost 19 cents each to mail bulk rate, the distribution cost is $190 for the mailing.

Mailing lists of all types can be bought. If the organization holding the meeting wishes to expand the number of people invited, it might buy a mailing list and send out an invitation to those on it. For example, a list of professors who study artificial intelligence might be purchased by the Association of Computer Research so that the professors could be invited to an ACR meeting.

Print costs vary. As mentioned, using colored ink and colored paper affects the cost of printed materials. A heavier weight of paper is not only more expensive, but can add to the cost of postage. Certainly the number of pages affects printing and postage costs. Printing on both sides of the paper doubles the printing cost but cuts the number of pages, thus reducing mailing weight and cost. Folding and binding (stapling) also add to print costs.

As more copies of an item are printed, the cost per copy generally goes down. For example, 1,000 copies of a flyer, printed on 60 lb. bond, one color, one side, costs approximately $69, or .069 cents each. If 1,500 copies of that same flyer are printed, the total cost is approximately $87,

Table 7.1 **Comparison of Printing Costs**

Paper Color	Paper Weight	Ink Color	Cost
White	60 lb.	Black	$53.42
White	60 lb.	Red	69.09
Blue	60 lb.	Black	55.39
Blue	60 lb.	Red	71.07
White	70 lb.	Black	56.05
Blue	70 lb.	Black	63.18

or .057 cents each. See Table 7.1 for the typical printing costs for 1,000 copies of a one-sided flyer.

The costs for promotional events include invitations, meals, and room charges (in other words, typical meeting costs). Occasionally a promotional event is sponsored and thus costs nothing for the meeting sponsor.

Telemarketing costs also vary. If professional telemarketers are hired for extensive telemarketing efforts, the planner should expect that there will be an hourly rate and an achievement bonus. To save money, members of the organization can be recruited to do the actual phoning.

Remember that for each meeting, the marketing strategy is different. A planner might utilize only one of these suggested methods, or all of them. The planner will often be responsible for designing the marketing plan, organizing the marketing materials, and overseeing the marketing effort. Following is a marketing checklist for meeting materials.

MARKETING CHECKLIST

Define the audience _____

_____

_____

Define the appeal of the meeting _____

_____

_____

Choose and schedule your marketing methods. A separate page may be needed for each planned activity.

DIRECT MAIL

Materials	Designed	Printed/ Obtained	Date Sent
Letter			
Stationery			
Invitation			
Brochure/Flyer			
Reservation form			
Hotel Reservation form			
Hotel materials			
Giveaways			

Airline discount flyer			
Rental car discount flyer			
CVB material			

ADVERTISING

Choose media for paid advertising.

Media	Publication Date	Deadline

PUBLICITY

Choose media for publicity/news releases. Establish a media list.

_____

_____

_____

_____

PROMOTIONAL EVENTS

Activity	Place	Date

TELEMARKETING PLAN

To Whom	Date	Personnel

CHAPTER ACTIVITY

Design a thorough marketing plan for an actual or imaginary meeting and fill out the Marketing Checklist. You may use the following sample meeting data to prepare the marketing plan and to select marketing materials and methods. Show any sample letters, flyers, brochures, advertisements, and news releases that you plan to use. You may use rough sketches or cut and paste from magazines to do this.

The Association of Independent Secondary School Business Managers is planning to hold its annual meeting in Las Vegas, Nevada, March 26–29, 19___. The meeting will be held at the Las Vegas Triple Palace Hotel. The membership totals 600. Last year's meeting drew 97 participants from across the nation.

Some of the topics to be covered are the new federal regulations concerning asbestos in schools, health insurance, retirement plans, liability insurance, and risk management. In spite of the seriousness of the meeting topics, the majority of people attend so that they can network with each other. During the three-day meeting, a dine-around is planned. A casino visit is also included the second night. A theme, "Supporting Education" has been chosen. Ten exhibitors from banks, insurance companies, and health care companies will display their materials. As the meeting planner you are very anxious to top last year's attendance figures. Outline your preferred marketing plan, including methods and timing.

Meeting Materials

Upon completion of this chapter,
you will be able to:

1. Determine what kinds of materials to prepare for a meeting

2. Estimate the quantities of materials needed

3. Suggest design factors for printed material

A t some meetings and exhibits, you see participants struggling with huge shopping bags full of brochures, booklets, flyers, invitations, notices, vouchers, and other materials. At others, participants seem only to have one four-by-eight inch program tucked in their pocket or purse.

Besides marketing materials, other materials are prepared for distribution or use at the meeting itself. They must be organized, designed, typed, printed, ordered, and distributed. Usually these items are prepared by the meeting planning staff prior to the meeting; sometimes, however, materials must be prepared during the meeting.

Nearly all meetings, for example, will require a registration form and a printed agenda or program. Most will require attendee lists, if only for accounting purposes. When participants do not know each other, nametags will be appreciated. If an exhibition or trade show accompanies a large meeting or convention, a list of exhibitors, vendors, and sponsors will be required. If admission is required for certain meeting-related events or if a meal count is required, tickets must be printed. If the meeting activities are held at several properties, transportation vouchers may have to be distributed. Signs will ensure that meeting "traffic" from banquet rooms to seminar rooms flows smoothly. Chapter 8 explains how to prepare these different kinds of meeting materials.

Registration/Reservation Forms

These forms are part of the marketing package and are commonly sent out with pre-meeting materials. Prior to the meeting, the purpose of the form is to reserve space. At the meeting, the form confirms how many people are present and how many chairs and meals are needed. It also provides information to the planner about auxiliary services, such as ground transportation during the meeting. For meetings where walk-ins with no prior reservations are expected, the registration form should be available at the registration desk. (See Chapter 9 for information on managing reservations and registration.)

What information is needed on the meeting reservation form? Usually, the following data is requested.

❑ **Full name.** The form may ask for the way a person wants his or her name to appear on a nametag.

❑ **Organizational or business affiliation.** If this is a corporate meeting of the ABC Widget Company at which everyone is from the same company, then the person's organizational affiliation is not needed. Nor would organizational or business affiliation be important to know for common interest attendees at the Chrysanthemum Growers annual convention.

❑ **Address.** Request both home and business address if needed.

❑ **Phone.** Both home and business phone numbers, plus **FAX** numbers, are asked for if appropriate.

❑ **Arrival and departure dates.** These indicate whether a person will attend the entire meeting and might also affect transportation arrangements.

❑ **Sessions or meals the person plans to attend.** A registration form may be used to sign the meeting participant up for the sessions she or he wishes to attend. It might also ask whether a person is planning to join the group for meals.

❑ **Gender and/or with whom the person will room with.** This information is for the meeting planner if roommates are to be assigned. Someone named Chris or Pat can be female or male. Some participants know in advance with whom they would prefer to share a room. Some planners also ask whether the person smokes.

❑ **How payment will be made.** There may be a registration fee, which reserves a participant's place at a meeting. This information is not needed if a company is paying for the expenses, but at most association meetings, individuals pay their own fees or different employers pick up the tab for their employees who attend.

Information about means of payment may be a "payment enclosed" box or may include space for a credit card number, expiration date, and signature.

Information on the registration card can help round out the participant profile. By simply adding demographic questions such as type of company, number of employees, or even food and recreation preferences, a planner receives data for the profile.

Figure 8.1 shows a sample meeting registration form.

Tomorrow's Office
sponsored by
The Business Education Association

June 7, 8, and 9, 19__

Name _____

Affiliation _____

Address _____

City/State/ZIP _____

Work phone _____ FAX _____ Home phone _____

Method of payment: ☐ Check ☐ Cash Other _____

Are you staying at the Sterling Plaza?   ☐ Yes ☐ No

Number of nights _____

Figure 8.1 **Sample Meeting Registration Form**

Programs and Agendas

The purpose of a meeting program is to inform and to guide attendees through the meeting. Among other things, the program describes the meeting sessions and gives times and locations for them. Even at small meetings, there should be typed agendas for attendees. A program may also be used as a marketing tool, and the planner may print several during the planning process. These tentative programs may be somewhat different from the final program given out at the meeting.

A program can be a simple, straightforward printed page giving only three pieces of information: what, when, and where. The agenda for the meeting of a board of directors may simply list the order of business—approval of the minutes from the last meeting, committee reports, financial reports, new and old business.

On the other hand, programs can be quite elaborate. They can include pictures and biographies of the speakers. The program can also include outlines of the various sessions and the speakers' notes and handouts for individual sessions. Professional papers might be reprinted in a program. In this case, the planner contacts speakers to request their papers and reprints them as proceedings. Paid advertisements may be sold in the program.

Exhibitors and sponsors of receptions or other meeting activities are usually listed prominently in the program as a way of acknowledging their contributions. If there are many exhibitors and sponsors, a separate list is a good idea.

The items that are included in the program determine its size and design. Obviously the more information that is included in the printed program, the more pages are required. When speakers' outlines, notes, handouts, photos, and biographies are included, the program might be softbound, like a paperback book. Many meeting sponsors will provide three-ring binders to the participants to hold all of the printed material for the meeting.

Binders can be customized with the meeting name, logo, dates, and location. Sometimes an outside organization, such as a Chamber of Commerce, is happy to provide a three-ring binder if advertising is allowed, particularly on the outside cover.

Even for simple programs, the planner must remember that a distinctive logo and colored paper and ink can strengthen the program design and contribute to the participants' perception that the meeting is a special event.

Obviously, the number of programs to print depends on the number of attendees expected at the meeting. The meeting planner should count the numbers of registrants, speakers, special guests, on-site meeting staff, and projected walk-in registrants in calculating how many programs to print. If the program is used as a direct mail marketing took, a sufficient number of programs must be printed to send to people on the mailing list.

The planner should anticipate that people will lose their programs.

Many will need several copies of the program—one to submit with a request for reimbursement, one for the Internal Revenue Service. Programs may be sent to the media, and sometimes programs are sent to people who do not attend the meeting. Therefore, at least 10% more than the number of programs minimally needed should be printed.

Nametags

"Hello, my name is . . ." is the universal nametag. It conveys identification. People meet and greet each other in elevators and in public rooms of the meeting property and recognize that they are attending the same meeting by their nametags. For this reason, the nametag takes on social importance.

Nametags can be used to distinguish certain meeting participants or to honor speakers or other guests. Many organizations have regular members and also associated or affiliated members. By using color codes or by adding the words "Speaker," or "Guest," these distinctions can be made.

The nametag can be used as proof of registration. People without may not be allowed into meeting sessions or meals. Nametags can further be used to divide the larger meeting group into smaller segments. For example, persons with yellow-bordered namecards go to Session 1 while others go to Session 2. Color codes and patterns on nametags can be used to indicate geographical divisions, chapter affiliations, and membership status, among other things.

Available in office supply stores, "hello tags" or their counterparts are sufficient for small or informal meetings. These are self-adhesive nametags, good for a one-day meeting. Usually people write their own names on the tag as they register; they may also list their business affiliations or any other pertinent information. Only the nametags, a pen, and a trash receptacle are needed.

Several other types of nametags are available. The most commonly used nametags are plastic sleeves into which a name card is slipped. They come with a variety of fasteners, often pins. However, the pins may make holes in clothing.

There are also plastic sleeves with elongated backs, designed to slip into a coat pocket. These are used mostly at all-male meetings where the gentlemen wear suitcoats or shirts with breast pockets. Plastic sleeves that have metal clips that swivel are probably preferable. They can be connected to a collar or a pocket, but many women's dresses have neither. The meeting planner should provide medium-sized safety pins that can be fastened beneath the fabric. The metal clip is then attached to the pin.

Certain chain or shoestring-type necklaces have hooks, slip latches, or slips with which to attach the nametag. For advertising purposes, a company's name or the meeting theme can be imprinted on the string. Unfortunately, these type of nametags swing freely, and the tag is often turned backwards. Many hang too low, so a person has to bend in order to read the nametag.

Most meeting planners order preprinted namecards that are inserted in the nametag holders. The meeting name, theme, and dates can be printed on the namecard, but costs can be lowered by purchasing generic nametags in quantity with just the organization name printed. These can be used for several meetings.

The size of the namecard must fit the plastic sleeve that is chosen, since sleeve sizes do vary. Also, if a computer is used to print names on the namecard, care must be taken that the size of the namecard is suitable for the printer. Six to eight namecards can be printed on a standard sheet of paper. Some printers can accommodate continuous feed namecards. Whatever the size of the namecard, however, the print must be legible and readable from a comfortable social distance.

As mentioned, people may write their own names on their namecards, but usually, namecards are prepared in advance. The registration form can ask people to specify how they want their names listed on the card.

Computer software can store registration information from which to print nametags. A variety of typefaces is available, and the size of the type can be adjusted. For example, WordPerfect 5.1 has these capabilities. Several other software packages are designed solely to make labels. Standard-size clear plastic labels can be purchased, printed on the computer, and adhered to the nametags, but this is time-consuming, so printing directly on the namecard is preferable.

Names can also be punched out on plastic strips, using a small machine that can be found in office supply and variety stores. The strips can be pasted to the nametags, but the letters are usually not very clear or visible. A calligrapher or graphic artist can be hired to write names on the nametags.

The meeting planner should expect to order enough nametags for the number of attendees expected plus five percent. As early registrations come in, a count can indicate whether to adjust the number to be printed. At the meeting, spare nametags should be available for walk-in registrations or lost nametags.

Participant Lists

One of the first things that people at a meeting want to know is "Who else is here?" They want to know if their friends, acquaintances, and business cohorts are also participating. Often a person has met someone at some other meeting and wants to know if that person is attending this meeting. Providing a list of participants meets these needs.

A participant list can be arranged alphabetically by last name. Business and home addresses and phone numbers can be shown. Because certain groups are interested in knowing the companies or organizations that are represented at meetings, a list can also be organized alphabetically by organization name with the representative who is attending the meeting also named. Some organizations want attendees to be listed by state or geographical region. The most efficient attendee list furnishes lists organized in all three ways.

Participant lists are difficult for the meeting planner to prepare because they must be organized, typed, and printed at the last moment. Word processing makes this much simpler. A list can be updated and printed as needed.

Participant lists are seldom 100% accurate. Some people expected will not arrive at the meeting for one reason or another. Some walk-ins may not preregister. Sometimes a group has to substitute its representative or delegate to the meeting. Therefore, the final participant list is usually printed a few days before the beginning of the meeting. At the meeting, an addendum can be prepared to show additions, deletions, and corrections. The list is available at the registration or information desk.

Exhibitor/Sponsor Lists

If the meeting incudes a large exhibition or trade show, the exhibitors expect their names and organization to appear prominently in the program or in a separate list. The booth number or location of the exhibit is usually given on the list. Large trade shows can generate an entire magazine that might also include display advertising.

If an exhibitor has paid for space or if a sponsor has provided some service or item for the meeting, it has a right to expect a proper listing in the program. The meeting planner must double-check exact spelling and other information when listing these participants. The planner distributes these lists from the registration desk or at the trade show entrance.

Tickets and Vouchers

Admission to meals and certain sessions may require more control and identification than a nametag provides, so tickets are printed for these events. Sometimes meals or events cost extra and tickets must be sold for them. At most meetings, the cost of meals is included in the price of registration. The per-person cost of a banquet can be over $50, and the charge for an overage on the guarantee quite costly. Therefore, some control must be exercised so that only those who have paid enjoy them. If there is a dine-around where attendees go to one of several restaurants in a city, strict accounting must be exercised because the meeting sponsor pays according to the number of people who eat at each restaurant.

Some meeting sessions might be open only to members of a certain standing in the organization. For example, the subject of a session might be confidential and those who attend may have to meet security clearance standards. Tickets can be issued to assure that only those who have met the clearance standard attend the session. Sightseeing or entertainment activities may also require tickets or vouchers.

Spouses who accompany meeting participants are usually invited to attend some meals and functions. These companions may have to verify that they have paid for an event. Finally, individuals who attend only a few meeting functions, but who do not register for the entire meeting, can be issued some type of voucher to admit them into the meals or sessions for which they have paid.

Tickets or vouchers can simply be marked with the meal or activity for which they can be used (for example, "Breakfast, Monday, October 16," or "Museum Tour, Wednesday, October 18"). The meeting planning staff can collect tickets, or others can collect them as meals are served or activities enjoyed.

Rolls of tickets can be purchased. Different tickets can be used for different functions. For example, blue tickets can be used for lunches and red tickets for the closing banquet. If there is a drawing or lottery at the meeting, tickets of this type can also come in handy.

For some meals, sessions, or events, there may be a limited number of people that can be accommodated. Even when all meeting participants receive tickets, extra tickets must be printed because there will be some lost tickets. The registration or information desk must have a procedure to verify that a person who has lost tickets was, in fact, issued the tickets and be able to replace the tickets.

Invitations

Invitations to attend special events are sometimes issued to certain participants at a meeting. The special event might be a reception for the board of directors or a hospitality suite party. Often the organization sponsoring the event provides the invitations. If the meeting planning staff is responsible for printing invitations, the options are many, from simple photocopied, typewritten invitations to engraved, formal ones. The registration desk must be given the invitation list and clear instructions about distributing invitations if this has not been done in advance of the meeting.

Signs

Signs direct people or tell them that they are in the correct place. If several meetings are being held simultaneously at the meeting property, signs tell which organizations are meeting in which session rooms. Usually in the lobby, there is a push-letter sign that tells what meetings are going on within the property and in which rooms they are being held.

A sign with the name of the meeting sponsor should identify the registration desk. Many organizations have banners that are used for this purpose. A sign identifying the organization might also be attached behind the podium or headtable. A sign on the podium is not only attractive, but provides publicity. For breakout sessions, signs with the name of the session should be displayed in front of the session room entrance. If there is a panel discussion, it is often appropriate to have the panel members' names imprinted on namecards or signs that are placed before them on the speaker table.

At some meeting activities, tables are assigned and tent signs with a number are placed on each table. Signs may also be needed to designate sections of a room where teams or subgroups should meet. These style signs can be produced by hand with poster board and felt-tipped markers.

At exhibitions and trade shows, the meeting sponsor is usually expected to provide basic signs for the displays, usually of a standard size and design. Exhibitors generally provide their own more elaborate signs.

Most signs are prepared by the meeting planning staff prior to the meeting. Signs should incorporate the meeting logo and the same design as the marketing materials, programs, and nametags. The art used on the program can be enlarged for signs. A disadvantage to this is that if the date and theme of a meeting are included on the sign, it becomes obsolete at the end of the meeting. If only the name of the organization is included, the sign can be used again, but this is not as effective for giving meeting participants specific information.

The meeting property usually provides easels on which signs can be placed. For easels, an 18 by 30 inch sign fits nicely. Heavy cardstock should be used that will remain upright on an easel. Signs are appropriately displayed in the lobby area and at elevators, escalators, and stairs to direct participants to session rooms. Small arrow signs can be attached to meeting signs to point out directions.

Sign makers offer many materials—plastic, cardboard, fabric, foam—and typefaces for manufacturing signs. The meeting staff can produce adequate signs for a small or low-budget meeting with a felt-tipped marker, or press-on type, both of which are available in office supply stores. Some businesses and associations have office machines that can print letters large enough to be suitable for signs.

Other Materials

❑ For meetings, exhibitions, or trade shows where a great deal of printed material is to be distributed, a carrying bag or case can be supplied to attendees. Often a sponsor or trade show participant is happy to donate a carrying case. Bags of all types provide excellent advertising space. Sponsors may include promotional items such as pens, pencils, and pads in their carrying cases.

If only a few printed materials will be distributed, a two-pocket folder might be appropriate. It can contain the program, any handouts, and invitations. Material from the meeting can be filed in the folder.

❑ Evaluation forms for use during the meeting must be printed. These may be for individual sessions or for the entire meeting.

❑ Placecards may be needed for meal services. These may be required for all meeting participants or only for those seated at the headtable. Placecards can be printed with the meeting logo, and individual names can be handwritten on them. To add a touch of elegance to a formal banquet, the evening's menu might be printed and placed at each table setting.

❑ For meetings that do not include meals, providing a list of restaurants within the vicinity of the meeting property is helpful. The meeting planner may make recommendations based on personal experience, the CVB might have a list, or, with permission, a tour guide list might be reprinted.

Certain restaurants might wish to provide advertising coupons that can be used by meeting participants. Trade show exhibitors might supply announcements about their exhibits. The meeting planner does not have to print or provide these materials, but often does have to manage their distribution.

❑ For a large, multiproperty meeting, a map of the city, spotlighting the hotels where attendants are staying and the convention center, is needed. A diagram of the meeting hotel and the appropriate meeting rooms is also often needed.

❑ Some large meetings produce a daily newsletter that updates participants about meeting activities, changes in the meeting schedule, and other things. This requires personnel, office space, and making printing arrangements. How to distribute the newsletter must be determined. Possibly the hotel will place it in participants' boxes, but there may be a charge for this.

❑ Elaborate gifts and promotional items can be given to participants, depending on the nature of the meeting. For example, at the Southern Governors' Conference, each state represented tries to out-do the other in giving products to delegates. Peanuts from Georgia, peach jam from South Carolina, and hot sauce from Louisiana are customary treats. Candidates at political conventions may give hats and buttons to participants. Trade show exhibitors may want to distribute samples of their products.

❑ If the meeting attendee is given one of each of the items discussed in this chapter, he or she will be loaded down with pounds of material. Struggling with this extra weight when returning home is unpleasant. One last item that the meeting planner can provide is a box in which to send the materials home by a postal or delivery service, which can be offered free of charge or for a fee. Corrugated boxes and labels are required. People can pack their own material and self-address their packages. Often, the box is at its destination before the person arrives home. Providing this service makes an excellent impression on those attending the meeting.

Costs

A typewriter, copier, felt-tipped marker, and typing paper can provide basic meeting materials. Computer graphics, a copier that enlarges and reduces, clip art, colored paper, and stencils can help the meeting planning staff create more interesting meeting materials. Budgets that include funds for printing, artwork, and staff support enable the production of well-designed meeting materials, which definitely contribute to the meeting's success.

As discussed in Chapter 7, colored papers and inks, the finished size of item, the number of pages, collation, the paper quality, number of folds, and special treatments (die-cuts, embossing) all affect print costs.

When appropriate, the meeting planner should try to find a sponsor who will underwrite the costs of meeting materials. A company might want to pay for printing the program in order to get its advertisement on the back cover. Folders or carrying bags with sponsors' names might be donated. For certain meetings, these sponsorships add to the "value for money" feeling; for others, they are wrong. It may not be wise, for example, for an association's meeting to appear to be sponsored by certain potential contributors. The politics of a business might be opposed to an association's aims. Perhaps a corporation that is skirting environmental regulations may think it is good business to be generous to an association that monitors environmental issues. But the attendees at the meeting could feel an obligation to whatever organization is providing financial support for the meeting. The meeting planner has to use good judgment and discuss compromising situations with the association or business sponsoring the meeting.

The meeting planner should establish deadlines for producing meeting materials, for example, six months, three months, and one month prior to the meeting. The Marketing Checklist that follows is a form that the meeting planner can use to track the process of producing or obtaining printed materials for the meeting. It can also serve as a shipping or packing list.

MEETING MATERIALS CHECKLIST

Enter the target completion dates.

Item	No. Needed	Distribution Method	Design	Print Method	Date Completed
Registration/ reservation form					
Program/Agenda					
Nametags					
Namecards					
Participant list					
Trade show/ Sponsor list					
Tickets/Vouchers					
Invitations					
Folder/Notebook					
Signs					
Tablets/Giveaways					
Evaluation forms					

Contributed Materials	Obtained	Distribution Method
Hotel registration form		
City brochures		
Discount coupons		

CHAPTER ACTIVITIES

1. Your real or imaginary meeting is scheduled to be held September 15–19. Write up the schedule for producing your meeting materials.

2. Investigate printers in your area. Write specifications (i.e., number of pages, size, color of paper and ink, number to be printed) for a real or imaginary program, and compare price quotes from two printers.

9

Reservations, Registrations, and Participant Services

Upon completion of this chapter, you will be able to:

1. Process meeting reservations and coordinate room reservations with the meeting property

2. Set up a registration desk

3. Organize VIP and hospitality suite management

4. Provide services for meeting participants, including information/messages and office support coordination

M eeting management is a numbers game, whether one is expecting 8 players for two tables of bridge or recording the 100,000 men, women, and children who attend a consumer electronics show. Reservations and registrations, the two Rs, give these numbers. Knowing the numbers is essential for arranging seating in meeting rooms, ordering meals, and crowd control at exhibitions. A meeting planner's nightmare is that bad weather closes an airport, causing late arrivals or no-shows or that more people than expected arrive for a meal.

For meetings, the terms *reservation* and *registration* are both used. The meeting registration is essentially a reservation for space at the meeting. It is an RSVP. Hotels use both a reservation card to reserve space and a registration card to process guests as they arrive at the property.

Property Reservations/Registrations

When the meeting site was chosen, the planner estimated the number of rooms needed. The property blocked, or reserved, them for the meeting dates. The date that the rooms would be released and the deadline for receiving the meeting discounted rate were also set at that time.

Pre-meeting Activities

For business meetings where attendance is essentially mandatory, the meeting planner usually makes all room reservations. In such a situation, the planner is able to confirm with the property the exact numbers and types of rooms needed. The meeting planner may decide who is to room with whom and may give the property a rooming list. The hotel assigns room numbers.

If the meeting organization will be paying the room charges, either for all attendees or just for speakers and important guests, the meeting planner will have to negotiate cancellation and refund policies in the property contract. The planner will usually make the room reservations as well. These charges will appear later on the master account for the entire meeting.

For most meetings, however, attendees make their own room reservations. Usually the meeting property provides a reservation card that is sent to attendees, who then return it to the hotel directly. Properties that are a part of a hotel chain may have toll-free telephone numbers that can be used by participants to make reservations.

Hotels often give a reservation number or confirmation number to those making reservations, which can be used when participants check in to trace reservations. Most hotels ask for a guarantee if a guest is going to arrive after a certain time, usually 4 P.M. or 6 P.M. The guarantee is usually for the first night's room fee; it is most often paid by credit card. A sample reservation card is seen in Figure 9.1.

On-Site Activities

At most meetings, people check into their rooms at the front desk. A front desk clerk confirms the person's reservation and asks him or her to fill out a hotel registration card. The clerk verifies how the hotel bill will be paid. The front desk should always be notified when a speaker or other person is to have a complimentary room.

Next, a room key is given to the meeting participant. At this time, the person may be directed to the official meeting registration desk. Sometimes the front desk distributes meeting materials as participants check in.

Generally, people arrive for a meeting within the same four-hour span before the first meeting session. Consequently, the front desk can be quite crowded and busy. For large meetings, a hotel sometimes sets up an adjunct front desk that serves only the attendees of a particular meeting. Although the hotel wants to serve those who attend a convention, it must also continue to serve its other guests.

Occasionally the meeting sponsor assists with hotel registration. The hotel assigns rooms and supplies a rooming list and room keys to the meeting planning staff. Upon arrival, participants register for their hotel rooms and for the meeting at the same time. The meeting planning staff distributes hotel registration cards and meeting registration forms if this has not been

```
                            RESERVATION CARD
  The
  Wise Hotel
  123 Berwinkle Blvd
  Los Angeles, CA 90077-1024
  1-213-555-2397                  RESERVATION NUMBER  98703
  ARRIVAL September 3, 19--       RESERVATION DATE Aug. 27, 19--
  DEPARTURE September 5, 19--     VIA phone
  NUMBER OF GUESTS 2              AGENT
  TYPE OF ROOM Twin               CONFIRMED
  RATE $40 per night              GUARANTEED       ✓


  NAME Ms. Jean Jennings
  ADDRESS 6918 Wynne Court
          Augusta, Georgia 30813-1024
  COMPANY Lyon Chemicals, Inc.
  WORK PHONE 404-555-2353   HOME PHONE 404-555-1111
  METHOD OF PAYMENT Plus credit card
```

Figure 9.1 Sample Hotel Reservation Card

done. Sometimes one form can be used for meeting and room registration, but most hotels prefer to use their own room registration forms.

Meeting Reservations/Registrations

The registration card supplies valuable information to the planner. For example, knowing when someone will be arriving at the airport can help arrange ground transportation to the property. The card may have asked for individual sessions that a person will attend. This helps the planner tell the property staff how many chairs to place in a meeting room, how many meals to serve, and how many buses to order.

A registration card is usually mailed with the meeting materials to each prospective attendee (see Figure 8.1). Registration cards are usually returned to the meeting planner. An acknowledgement or confirmation of the registration card might be sent to the attendees. Most want confirmation that they are registered and that their payment was received. A packet of information containing program information, notes on transportation alternatives, a city brochure, and other materials may be sent out at this time. A confirmation letter might state, "Bring this letter with you. It serves as your registration confirmation."

It is not uncommon for a meeting sponsor to require that all or part of the meeting registration fee be paid in advance of the meeting. Often the price of registering is lower if paid before a certain date. For example, for a September 15 meeting, the registration cost may be $300 if paid by August 15 and $350 if paid after August 15. Registration fees give the planner cash flow with which to pay meeting staff and print meeting materials.

Registration cards are not usually sent when the names and numbers of participants are all but assured. For business meetings at which participation is mandatory, there is usually no registration fee.

How payment is made is vital to registration processing. Checks must be deposited, credit card vouchers completed and mailed to the credit card company, and purchase orders billed. A policy has to be established for extending credit.

As discussed in Chapter 7, the reservation information might be keyed into a computer, which will later be used to generate an attendee list and nametags. The reservation card itself should be filed alphabetically or by region.

There are companies that contract to handle reservations for meetings. They can usually take reservations with electronic mail, FAX, and toll-free phone numbers. They usually have sophisticated computers that can manipulate extensive databases. Among other services, these companies will sometimes deposit registration payments. They can generate invoices and attendee lists and also produce nametags and admission tickets for meeting events. Such companies can run statistical reports, geographic and demographic analyses, and summary reports. These companies can transport their hardware and software to the meeting site. These contractors can also act as housing bureaus, managing multiple property reservations. Some CVBs own this type of equipment.

Figure 9.2 is a tally sheet that the meeting planner can use to track hotel and meeting reservations.

A week before the meeting opens, anticipation is high. The approach of "opening day" can be felt. Yet, a myriad of last-minute tasks must be performed by the meeting planning staff. During this time, the meeting planner must be in especially close contact with the meeting property personnel.

Getting the Materials to the Meeting

At the headquarters or home office of the meeting organization, the business office environment with its materials, office supplies, and files must now be virtually transferred to the meeting site. Meeting planning staff will surely feel as if they are packing a household of goods to be sent to the meeting site. Exact instructions and information must be given to the meeting property concerning the number and type of shipments that will be arriving. Ask specifically where meeting materials will be stored.

Registration and Tally Sheet

Meeting _____

Date _____

Meeting Registrations

Date	Weekly Total	Cumulative Total	

Hotel Reservations

Date	Weekly Total	Cumulative Total	Block Remaining

Figure 9.2 **Registration and Reservation Tally Sheet**

All of the materials mentioned in Chapter 8 must be packaged and transported to the meeting. This includes nametags, programs, giveaways, directories, signs, and other items. Each box of materials should be numbered and inventoried. For international meetings, allow two months for surface mail and be sure to complete customs declarations. The Meeting Materials Checklist on page 114 can be used for this purpose with an additional column indicating when the materials were sent.

Some meeting materials, such as the program, can be sent directly from the printer to the meeting site. Printers and other suppliers must be given exact information on how to address packages so that the property will safeguard them for the meeting sponsor. Although letting suppliers handle materials seems convenient, it may not be worth the anxiety of checking with the property as to whether the materials have arrived.

When to send the materials is crucial. No one can guarantee delivery times even though overnight package service is more or less reliable. Certainly meeting materials must arrive at the meeting site before people arrive to register. On the other hand, if the meeting materials arrive too early, they may fall into the hands of front desk personnel or property staff who do not know that the meeting is scheduled and who may return the materials to the sender.

Some meeting planners choose to send office supplies that might be needed during a meeting, although hotels and other meeting properties are able to supply some of them. By having many of these supplies on hand, the meeting planner can save a great deal of time and aggravation, not to mention cost. To avoid transporting these items, office supplies may also be purchased from an office supply company in the meeting city. The following checklist shows the kinds of office supplies that may be needed at a meeting.

OFFICE SUPPLY CHECKLIST

- ❑ Typewriter
- ❑ Computer
- ❑ Typing/computer paper
- ❑ Extra ribbons
- ❑ Correction fluid
- ❑ Message pads
- ❑ Pencils/Pens
- ❑ Scissors
- ❑ Cash drawer
- ❑ Receipt book
- ❑ Thumbtacks
- ❑ Hammer
- ❑ Masking/plastic/rug tape

- ❏ Screwdriver
- ❏ Pliers
- ❏ Stapler/Staples
- ❏ Paper clips
- ❏ Masking tape
- ❏ Felt-tipped markers
- ❏ Poster board
- ❏ Tape measure

Managing the Registration Desk

At the meeting, the responsibility of the meeting planning staff changes from planning to executing the meeting. Overseeing the meeting sessions, registration and communications with the property staff are among the many activities. The registration desk becomes the coordinating point.

Setting Up

For conventions at which participants may be staying at several properties, one of the hotels or the convention center might be the registration site. A bank of tables can be set up and attendees directed to the proper line alphabetically by their last name initial, member status, or some other criterion.

It is important to have adequate space for registration activities. For large meetings, a ballroom might be needed for registration. For single-property meetings, the registration desk is usually given a prominent location within the hotel. This might be the main lobby or ideally it is set up in a hallway or public area near the meeting rooms.

Usually tables are used for registration desks. For the sake of appearance, they should be draped with a cloth. A banner or some type of sign that reads "Registration" and the name of the organization or meeting can be attached to the table. Placing flowers on the registration desk is a nice touch, and balloons tied to the desk attract attention.

Meeting materials such as programs and giveaways can either be kept under a skirted table and handed out individually, or they can be placed on the table for attendees to pick up. Often, nametags are laid out in alphabetical order so that attendees can locate them. City brochures, flyers, and coupons can also be kept on the table.

The meeting planner should work with the hotel engineering department beforehand if registration activities require office machines. The appropriate supports and power supplies should be provided. If an outside contractor has handled reservations, it will usually bring in equipment and organize its setup. Ideally, a house phone can be hooked up at the registration desk. A phone enables the meeting staff to call various hotel departments, keep in touch with other organizational staff, and contact meeting participants. A phone at the registration desk is also a service to meeting participants who want to contact each other without going to a public phone or returning to their rooms. If an outside line is available on the registration desk phone, the meeting planner must authorize who can use the phone and who pays for calls made to outside numbers.

The hotel switchboard will probably route incoming calls to participants to the registration desk. The meeting planner decides how to handle messages that are for meeting participants. Generally, messages can be tacked to a bulletin board.

The hotel should be asked to provide sufficient wastepaper baskets at the registration desk. It should also provide a pitcher of water, glasses, and a list of departmental extensions for registration personnel.

Staffing

The hours that the registration desk operates must be selected. Usually, the desk is open a half day prior to the opening session of the meeting to accommodate early arrivals. Normal hours may be 4 P.M. to 9 P.M. in the evening before opening day and 7 A.M. to 6 P.M. on opening day. On subsequent days, the registration desk can open 30 minutes prior to opening session.

Registration formally ends when everyone with reservations has arrived and is accounted for, but most registration desks stay open throughout the meeting.

Who will staff the registration desk must be determined. Most often, the organization's support staff goes to the meeting and acts as the meeting staff. People who work 9 A.M. to 4:30 P.M., Monday through Friday, will find registration desk hours much longer. Thus, meeting budgets may have to reflect overtime pay or compensatory time off.

Some organizations may have too few staff members to deploy for meeting activities, including registration. Temporary help can be hired or contracted for at the meeting site. Some companies' sole purpose is to supply temporary convention staff, but these companies are usually found only in cities that host numerous conventions. Many CVBs have part-time staff that is available for meeting registration. These arrangements should be negotiated well before the meeting takes place. Volunteers or hotel personnel might be another source of meeting staff.

Some meetings may require interpreters at the registration desk. A bonded cashier, and possibly an armored guard for bank delivery, also may be necessary if much money will be exchanged during registration. A person might be appointed to greet people. Another person may be asked to supervise the registration lines. Someone in authority should be present and easily accessible at the registration desk at all times.

Meeting registration basically involves verifying that a meeting participant has registered and paid for the meeting. If everything is in order, registration staff then distribute meeting materials, including tickets and vouchers, to the participant. It is important to keep accurate tallies as items are distributed. Eventually, these tallies will be used to give accurate attendance figures for meals and special events.

Even though most participants will have prepaid their registration fees, cash may be received either from attendees who did not preregister or from walk-ins. If these people can be accommodated at the meeting, their fees are collected and they are given their meeting material.

A "bank" may need to be established. This is cash taken to the meeting in order to be able to make change. Safety deposit boxes are available at front desks and should be used to safekeep cash. Large amounts of cash may require armored truck pick-ups.

Additionally, any number of odd jobs might be the responsibility of the registration desk personnel. These can be as tedious as placing a folder on each participant's seat in breakout rooms or as fun as doing special deliveries and hospitality room setup.

Meeting staff may also be called on to distribute materials such as flowers, wine, or a fruit basket to speakers and important guests. The hotel provides a list of room numbers and keys so that the meeting staff and a bellperson can deliver the items to the rooms.

Further, the meeting staff opens, and sometimes staffs, hospitality suites during a meeting. Arrangements may have been made whereby the hotel stocks these suites with food and drink, or the meeting staff might stock them. Flower arrangements should be ordered for these rooms. To execute all of these tasks, the registration staff must be well trained.

Staffing schedules must be established, taking into account peak times for registration. It may be most efficient to assign duties such as delivering messages or providing city information. Certain procedures, such as those for handling partial registrations, individual meal tickets, or direct billing, must be established and reviewed.

Dress codes and whether mingling with participants is permitted may be covered. How to address participants—using last names only, using titles—should be discussed. It never hurts to give a pep talk. Remind registration staff to be friendly and to remember that participants are at a special event at which they are entitled to expect courteous and competent service.

Finally, registration desk staff should be instructed about what to do in an emergency. They should know where emergency exits are located. They should also have a list of emergency phone numbers.

REGISTRATION CHECKLIST

Location of registration desk or area _____

Registration desk design

    Signs _____

    Tablecloth _____

    Flowers _____

    Other decorations _____

    Equipment (phone, typewriter, computer, message board) _____

    _____

    Meeting materials provided (list) _____

    _____

Staffing

    Who _____

    _____

    Wages _____

    _____

    Scheduling _____

    _____

    Duties assigned: (greeter, messenger, information desk) _____

    _____

    Meeting Materials Checklist (Chapter 8)

        Person assigned responsibility _____

    Office Supply Checklist

        Person assigned responsibility _____

    Training (include deportment and dress code) _____

    □ Emergency procedures reviewed?

    □ Registration staff introduced to hotel personnel?

Policies and procedures

    Cash handling _____

    Safety deposit box _____

    Transferring to a bank _____

    Change taken _____

    Billing (group discounts, purchase orders) _____

    Individual sessions/meals _____

    Nonmembers _____

    Partial registration _____

    Complimentary registration (press, presenters) _____

    Refunds _____

    Replacing tickets and vouchers _____

    Phone procedures _____

    Message delivery method _____

Serving Participants

Once the formal registration activities are complete, the registration desk turns into a service desk with important functions to perform during the meeting.

Producing and Replacing Meeting Materials

If a participant list has not been previously prepared before the meeting, it must be organized and made available at the meeting. An addendum to the attendants list might be typed, copied and distributed. An updated list, including hotel room numbers, might be produced.

An amazing number of adults will lose their meeting materials. Certain items, such as gifts or expensive giveaways, cannot be replaced, but certainly replacement programs, attendee lists, or exhibitors lists can be supplied. When replacing nametags, tickets, and vouchers, great care should be taken to ensure that only the person who is entitled to such materials receives them.

Taking Messages

As mentioned, the hotel switchboard may route incoming calls to meeting participants, and participants may want to contact each other. A bulletin board can be used to post messages. Phone message notepads can be used for this. They can be folded so that only the name of the person for whom the message is intended shows. Meeting room or schedule changes can be posted on the message board. A local business, such as a restaurant, may ask to place a promotional flyer on the board.

Providing Information, Referrals, and Other Services

A service desk will ordinarily be asked for information about the meeting itself and about the convention town. "Where is the Session II meeting room?" "What time is the banquet tonight?" "When does Joe Jones speak?" Most of the information requested about the meeting can be answered by simply referring to the meeting program and the meeting staff having been familiarized with the hotel floor plan.

"Where can I get this heel replaced?" "Where is the nearest pizzeria?" "Is the ballet presenting The Nutcracker tonight?" To answer questions about a city such as these, a phone book, tourist guides, a city directory, and a newspaper are handy.

The service desk is the lost and found center. The bulletin board can be used to announce lost and found items. If a lost item is very valuable, the hotel security department should be notified.

Last, the registration desk might serve as a office center for the use of the attendees. At some meetings a separate room is set up with computers, typewriters, a FAX service, copying machines, and even secretarial staff. Many properties have office centers that provide equipment and personnel services for a fee.

Packing up

One last extra that the service desk can provide was discussed in Chapter 8. Boxes and labels can be supplied so that meeting participants can send meeting materials to their homes or offices. Individuals pack, tape, and address their parcels. The registration staff either mails them or arranges for a delivery service to pick them up. This is an ultimate service that leaves a good impression.

Working with the Property Staff

The registration/service desk is the core of communications with the hotel. The hotel usually assigns a meeting manager or convention services manager (CSM) to coordinate the meeting with the meeting planning staff. Often meeting planners will be given walkie-talkies with which to keep in contact with the hotel staff during the meeting. (See Chapter 10 for more information on working with the property staff.)

Furnishing certain information or services will require working closely with particular departments of the hotel. Prior to the meeting, key meeting staff personnel should introduce themselves to the managers of each department. Final meal counts are conveyed to the catering department. The engineering department is consulted for meeting room arrangements. The housestaff sets up tables and chairs.

CHAPTER ACTIVITIES

1. Design a meeting registration card that will obtain all the information you deem necessary for record keeping, fiscal accountability, and making up a participant list for the Teachers of Typing meeting.

2. List the participant services that would be most appropriate for the Teachers of Typing meeting, and rank them according to their importance (for example, message board, copying capability).

3. Develop a procedure to handle money at a meeting.

Meeting in Progress

Upon completion of this chapter,
you will be able to:

1. Choose the appropriate room design for specific sessions
2. Design the head table and backdrop
3. Coordinate audiovisual meeting requirements

"The best laid plans of mice and men oft times go awry" is very true of meeting session management. This chapter is about the heart of the meeting—on-site session management. Good planning is important, but on-the-spot decisions, many of which may seem trivial, will have to be made. Many of these decisions are integral to the success of the meeting.

Some planning decisions will be made by the meeting planner and the meeting sponsor many months, or years, in advance of the meeting. Some are made by consulting with the meeting property. Other decisions, such as whether smoking will be restricted or which doors to close, may be made by the meeting planner only minutes before the meeting opens.

Session Management

Working with the Property Staff

The meeting planner's counterpart on the property staff is the convention services manager (CSM). At the same time that the planner is working to represent the organization's best interests in terms of planning and executing a meeting that will help the organization achieve its objectives, the CSM is working to ensure that the meeting goes off without a hitch—that rooms are properly set up, that the kitchen prepares the correct number of meals, that the accounting department knows what charges are billed to individuals and which to the organization.

It is usually the larger meeting properties that employ CSMs, but the planner should expect that most properties will designate one person outside of their sales department on whom the planner can rely during the meeting to resolve problems. The CSM is paid to assist the planner, not to resist the planner.

The basis of the planner's relationship with the CSM is cooperation. An example of how this cooperation was realized between one planner and a CSM was when prior to a meeting, the CSM pointed out that a dance floor was laid down for a dinner dance to be held in a particular meeting room that evening. The planner, who had rented a carpeted room, could have demanded that the dance floor be removed entirely, but instead requested that only one small section, which presented a safety hazard, be removed. The CSM was honest in pointing out the error. The planner was flexible. Mutual respect was established. The property staff was grateful that its job had been made simpler and did many favors for the planner afterward.

A planner usually contacts the CSM with meal counts, changes in room setups, requests for additional water and coffee, additional seating, and any number of special requests. It is helpful to have a house phone available at the registration desk so that calls to the CSM can be made quickly. As mentioned, some properties provide beepers or pagers.

Occasionally, a planner will directly contact the banquet manager or the head of the house staff, engineering, or housekeeping departments with requests. An order for an additional urn of coffee can go directly to the catering department. A request for an additional table at the registration desk can go directly to the house staff. The planner and the CSM should decide which requests are to be directed to the CSM and which should be brought to the appropriate department head. When these requests are likely to incur costs, it is usually best to deal with the CSM.

Probably the most frequent calls to the CSM during a meeting are to request temperature changes in the meeting rooms. It always seems to be too hot or too cold for some people. When the planner hears consistent complaints about temperature, the CSM should be called. Often nothing can be done. When the lights are lowered for slides or films, the room gets colder. If only a few people are in a large room, the room gets colder. Conversely, a crowd will literally heat up a room.

The CSM also can serve as concierge. He or she can put the planner into contact with the correct person to handle special requests. The CSM might pave the way for someone to cash a personal check or, perhaps, to get group theater tickets.

Working with the Session Chair

Undeniably, the meeting planner bears some responsibility for the outcome of the meeting. But simply having a good working relationship with the property staff and well-appointed function rooms does not guarantee success. Because the planner cannot possibly be everywhere at once, he or she must know when to share the load of session management.

Successful meetings have session chairs, or people who are in charge of each meeting session. The session chair usually introduces the speaker or panelists, acts as a moderator, coordinates with the audiovisual equipment operator, and calls time when the session should end.

The meeting planner should brief the session chairs about their duties and responsibilities. They should be informed if there is another meeting immediately following their particular session so that they can keep the program on schedule. The planner can supply the session chairs with electronic timers or stoplights. The planner should also ask the session chairs to make general announcements, including information concerning the next session. The Session Chair Responsibility Checklist summarizes the duties of a session chair.

SESSION CHAIR RESPONSIBILITY CHECKLIST

❑ Meet with speaker(s) to determine needs

❑ Obtain speaker(s) biographies

❑ Distribute materials for session

❑ Introduce session, stating objectives

❑ Introduce speaker(s)

❑ Oversee audiovisual operation

❑ Control lighting/heating/cooling

❑ Close sessions at appropriate time

❑ Distribute and collect evaluations

Notes _____

_____

_____

Setting Policies

The meeting planner will often have to take the lead in formulating policies that regulate behaviors and activities that affect everyone's comfort at the meeting. In doing so, the planner will be exercising his or her communication skills to the utmost.

For example, the smoking issue must be addressed by the planner. The trend now is to designate smoking areas. Most meetings do not allow smoking within the meeting session rooms, and more and more meal events separate smokers from nonsmokers. The planner should understand that when holding very large meetings, it may be impossible to arrange for a totally smoke-free space if the property is hosting other groups that permit smoking.

The meeting planner must also decide if announcements of phone calls are to be made during meeting sessions. At a meeting of 200 people, a great deal of the meeting time could be taken up with messages such as "Mr. Jones, please call your office" and "Ms. Smith, it's urgent that you call the district office." Many people love to hear their names announced and some people will even stage such "urgent" messages. It is preferable to post messages on the message board.

Finally, ground rules may need to be set for the media. Photographers provide coverage of the meeting for the public, common interest groups, and individuals. For highly publicized events, photographers are usually courted. Association meetings may rely on publicity, enhanced by photographs, to get the word out about the significance of their meetings and objectives. In any case, photography shouldn't interfere with or detract from the actual meeting. Set rules about the use of cameras and communicate them to individuals, news media, and contracted professionals.

Function Room Design

The draft program, discussed in Chapter 4, shows how many function rooms are required and when they are needed. At the first meeting with the property staff, the planner chooses which function rooms will be used. This information then is spelled out in the contract with the hotel. A typical contract might specify a ballroom for general sessions, smaller rooms for breakout sessions, space for meals, and perhaps a two-bedroom suite for hospitality.

Even experienced planners rely on function sheets, which compile information about how a meeting room should be set up for a particular session, how refreshments should be served, what audiovisual equipment is required, and other details. Usually, the meeting property will send a function room sheet to the planner. (See Figure 10.1).

As with all other meeting materials, the function sheet should be filled out accurately. For large meetings, function sheets may be prepared months in advance of the actual meeting. They should be updated if information changes. For smaller meetings, function sheets might be prepared only a week or two before the meeting. However, if the property has promised to provide special services or equipment, the meeting planner should not wait until the last minute to find out whether they are available.

When booking function rooms, the planner should consider what they will be used for and inspect them very carefully. The location of windows and doors, for example, is important. A room with an unshaded window will be unsuitable for showing films. Pillars or columns may block some audience members' view of the stage. Electrical outlets should be conveniently located. Lighting and seating should be conveniently located. Lighting and seating arrangements should be adequate. These factors and others are discussed below.

Doors

The first major element in meeting room design is its doors. How many are there? Is at least one door wide enough for a person using a wheelchair or walker? If there are several doors, the planner should decide which ones to use. Often the door closest to the podium is blocked as a courtesy to

Date _____   Time _____

Room _____   Number of people _____

Organization _____   Name of meeting _____

Person in charge _____   Headquarters room _____

Function Room Setup and Design

Head table _____ Number of people _____ Riser _____

Number of microphones _____ Placement _____

Number of chairs _____ Schoolroom _____ Auditorium _____

Water service _____

Food service _____

Menu _____

Service style _____

Equipment   Pads _____   Pencils _____   Ashtrays _____   Other _____

Audiovisual Equipment

Type and number of microphones _____

Microphone locations _____

Podium _____

Lectern _____

Easel/flipchart _____

Chalkboard _____

Projection equipment _____

Tape recorder/cassette recorder _____

Other _____

Room Diagram

Figure 10.1 **Sample Function Sheet**

speakers to eliminate possible distractions. If films or slides are being projected, closing the doors nearest the screen enhances the picture quality.

Fire codes may preclude locking or blocking doors completely, in which case signs simply stating, "Please do not open during sessions," have to suffice. It may be permissible to use barriers, however. Chairs, the registration desk, a refreshment table, or an easel with a sign on it can be employed as barriers. Remember to block doors both on the inside and the outside.

If a meeting restricts attendance, it is best to block all but one entrance. Someone can check credentials as participants enter the meeting room.

Head Table and Podium

The second major element in room design is the location of the head table or podium. Most rooms are rectangular; the speaker stands at one end, looking lengthwise down the room. If a head table faces the width of the room, the speaker has to turn to make eye contact with the audience. The head table or podium should be at least six feet from the first row of tables or chairs.

If an audiovisual presentation is to be part of the program, the location of the head table or podium may be predetermined by the location of film screens or electrical outlets. Fortunately, newer properties usually have sufficient outlets to give the planner flexibility in this regard. The audiovisual requirements of a meeting are discussed later in this chapter.

Elevating the head table or podium with risers or by placing it on a stage puts speakers in better view of their audience. For entertainment events, a stage's best placement may be in only one location. Security requirements for public figures can limit the choice of where a stage or podium is located. Direct access might be required from a door to the podium.

A head table should be long enough to comfortably seat the number of speakers, panelists, or dignitaries who will be sitting there. There should also be enough room in front of and in back of the chairs at the head table so that no one is seated too close to the edge of a stage and so that people can walk easily from the table to a lectern or stand-up microphone.

A center podium may be used, or podiums with microphones may be placed on either end or on both ends of the head table. The podium should be placed to the side if a center screen is being used. If a center podium is chosen or if a tabletop lectern is used at a head table, it is good protocol to seat the host, president, executive director, senior partner, or conference chair in the center seat. The second most honored person or featured speaker sits to the right of the host. The third-ranking person sits to the host's left. Seating proceeds right/left from the center seat. Figure 10.2 displays a classic head table design, with 1 being the most important person (host) and 7 being the least important person.

A head table may not be needed. Chairs can be placed before the audience for some presentations. If a standalone podium is used, ask the

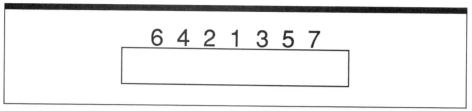

Figure 10.2 Classic Head Table Design

speaker if he or she would like to have a small stand or table beside the podium.

Some decoration on or behind the head table may be desirable. Flowers or signs with the organization or meeting name on it are appropriately placed in front of the podium. A sign on the podium or on the back wall provides publicity for the group or meeting if photographers are present. Flags may be displayed on the podium. If it is displayed, the national flag of the country in which the meeting is held should be to the right of either the host or the podium. If a flag is hung on a wall, its grommets should be on the left.

Lighting

Lighting is the third major element in room design. A room's lighting fixtures can control where the head table is placed and how the audience is seated. A bank of small spotlights, permanently installed in the ceiling, may shine where the head table is placed. If at all possible, lights should be placed so that speakers are not looking directly into them.

Using larger follow spotlights is an option for some meetings, particularly if there is activity on a stage. If multiple or movable spotlights are needed, scaffolding must be securely erected and a skilled lighting technician hired.

If slides, films, or videos are shown, the house lights will have to be dimmed. The planner should know where the controls are. A lighting rehearsal might be in order.

Refreshment Service

Refreshment service also figures into function room design. Water should be provided to participants in each function room. Pitchers and glasses can be set at intervals along the audience tables. People moving around to get water can be distracting, so for small meetings it is preferable to place pitchers and glasses on the audience tables. One pitcher can usually serve six to eight people.

Refreshments can also be set on service tables placed around the room. For a meeting of 250 people or more, at least four service tables should be set, each with six to eight pitchers and 50 to 60 glasses.

Some meetings do not have formal coffee or refreshment breaks, but coffee or refreshments are provided in the meeting room itself for people to help themselves. For a small meeting, one service table should do; for a larger one, several stations should be set up. Water should always be provided at the service tables.

Seating

Unless the seats are bolted to the floor, the planner must choose a seating arrangement for the room. This is the fifth major element in room design. For general sessions, the classic styles are *theater* and *classroom*. (See Figure 10.3.) The difference between them is that tables are used in classroom seating. For theater seating, nine to ten square feet per person is required. For classroom seating, 15 to 17 square feet per person is required.

The property staff can advise the planner on setups that will conform with local fire and safety regulations. For example, in large rooms, the center aisle should be six feet wide. In smaller rooms, though, the aisles could be four feet wide. Two aisles may be chosen, dividing the seating into thirds. Fire regulations may also require back and side aisles. Anyone who is using a wheelchair, walker, or crutches should have adequate room to maneuver.

People interact best when they face each other. Both classroom and theater arrangements permit face-to-face encounters between the audience and the speaker, but they do not allow participants to make eye contact with other audience members without turning. Classroom and theater arrangements also have the disadvantage of placing one person directly behind another, thus hindering vision. The *herringbone* or *V-shaped* arrangement shown in Figure 10.4 alleviates some of these problems. It can be used with or without tables.

Breakout rooms may be set up in either classroom style or theater

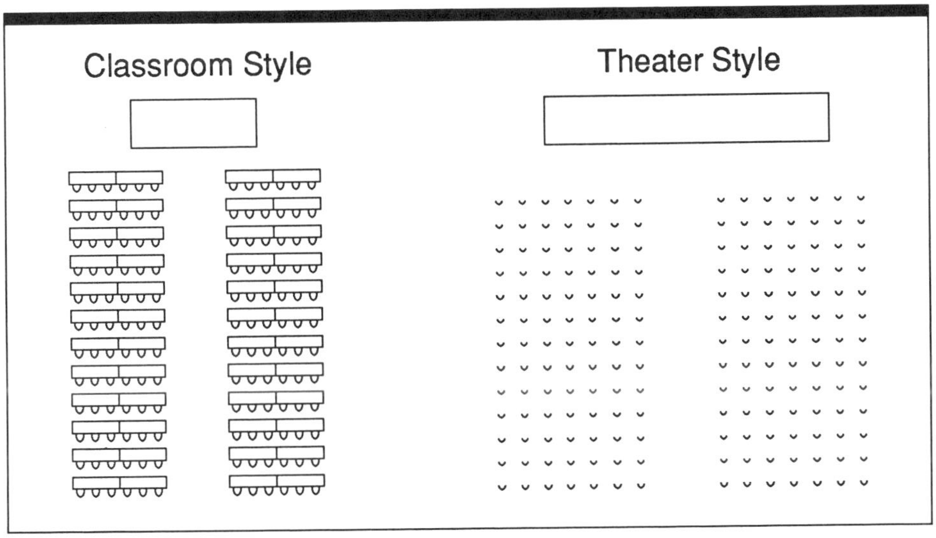

Figure 10.3 Classic Seating Designs

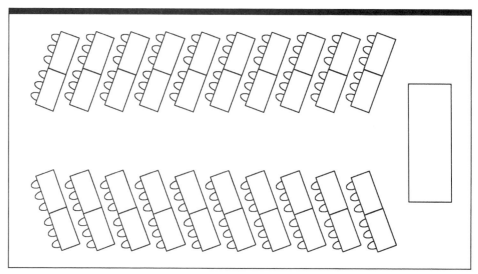

Figure 10.4 Herringbone Seating Design

style. Since there are usually fewer people than in general sessions and because breakout sessions invite more interaction between participants, other options can be considered, as shown in Figure 10.5.

The meeting planner can use the number of preregistrants as a guide for how many seats need to be set up. If people have preregistered for breakout sessions, the planner will have additional information about seating. Still, there may be walk-in registrations requiring additional seating.

If the room has been set up in classroom style and additional participants arrive, ask the house staff to remove the back two or three rows of tables and set chairs theater-style there. More people can be seated without the tables. If fewer participants attend than expected, the setup staff should be requested to remove the back rows. This forces people to move toward the front and does not leave them scattered around the room. A room that is half-full is also half-empty and gives a bad impression.

Other Elements

Setting up some function rooms involves more than attending to the major elements of entrances and exits, head table design, lighting, refreshment service, and seating arrangements. The text below summarizes some of the other elements that the planner must commonly consider.

Table Set-up

Both the head table and audience tables usually are draped or have tablecloths, placed so that the cloth hangs to the floor in the front and to waist level on the side where people are sitting, which shields legs and feet from view. The planner is usually asked to choose a tablecloth color.

Often the property provides and places writing tablets and pencils at each chair or table setting and small bowls of wrapped hard candy. Some-

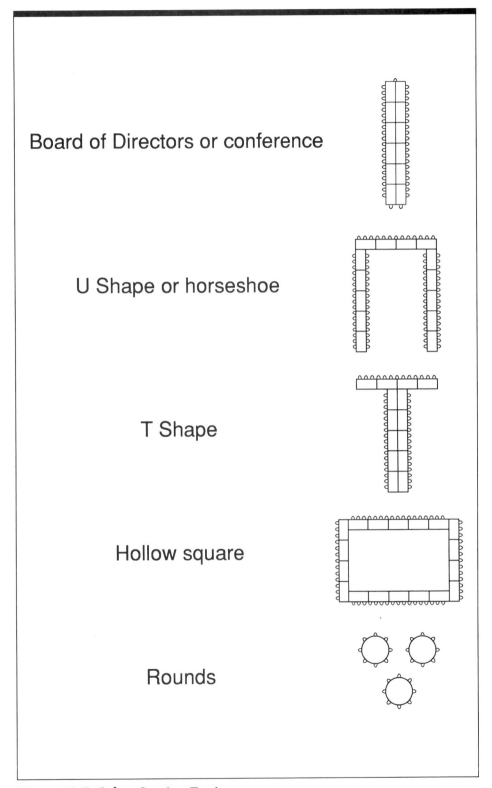

Board of Directors or conference

U Shape or horseshoe

T Shape

Hollow square

Rounds

Figure 10.5 Other Seating Designs

times the meeting organization provides giveaways or printed material for placement at each setting. The planner should schedule time and personnel to distribute these items.

Meal Service

Room setup can be the same as for breakout sessions or smaller individual oblong or round tables may be used. Oblongs may be joined end to end to seat any number of people (see the board of directors seating design in Figure 10.5). A standard oblong table is six or eight feet long and 18 to 30 inches wide. Two feet should be allowed per person for dining. Rounds may be five, six, or eight feet in diameter. A five-foot round can seat six to eight people, and a six-foot round can seat up to 10 people. (See Chapter 11 for more information on food and beverage service).

Room Set-up Timing

The setup and break-down time for meeting rooms has to be closely co-ordinated with the CSM. For example, a room cannot be set up in classroom-style (see Figure 10.3) until 12:00 noon and then set up in rounds (see Figure 10.4) for lunch at 12:30 P.M. Sometimes a room is set for both meeting sessions and meals, with the area towards the podium set classroom-style for the meeting and the back of the room set with rounds for lunch. Just be sure that tables are set before the commencement of a meeting, because the clang of flatware and glasses is distracting.

The planner should know if the property has sold the contracted space either before or after each session. If a session runs longer than the allotted time and the room has been sold back-to-back, it can be chaotic. Although the property's set up staff sometimes seem to perform miracles, there is a limit to their abilities. Perhaps the organization will pay extra to keep a room empty to assure that setup time is adequate.

An example of a tight schedule is a very formal meeting of 400 scientists set classroom-style in a ballroom that is followed by a high school prom set with rounds for dinner for 350 and a dance floor. The scientists' last session is due to end at 5:30 P.M. but runs over to 6:00 P.M. The first prom guests are due at 7:30 P.M. So, in but an hour and a half, 400 chairs must be removed, the speaker table dismantled, the audiovisual equipment stored, the classroom tables and stage removed, the rounds brought in and set up, 350 chairs placed, and the dance floor laid. Although the room change can occur in that time, it is stressful for everyone involved.

Adjunct Rooms

Besides the rooms in which sessions are held, the planner may contract for other rooms.

❑ **Press room.** A press room is usually established near the general assembly meeting room. Often it is a smaller meeting room with several electrical outlets for microphones and taping equipment. Tables and chairs are provided and a "Press Only" sign is posted. Typewriters or computers might be set up in the room. The hotel can provide outside telephone lines, though the average cost is $100 per day. (Alternatively, the press room could be located near public phones.)

If a press conference is to be held, a head table and classroom seating is appropriate. Some refreshments might be served at the back of the room. Customarily, a table is provided for handouts such as press releases.

❑ **Speaker-ready room.** A speaker-ready room is occasionally set aside so that speakers can have privacy to rehearse before their presentations. The room may have a slide previewer or caramate so that the sequences of slides can be confirmed. Three or four small round tables with chairs are a good arrangement for this room. This room can also be booked for the duration of the meeting and used to store materials safely when meetings are not in session.

❑ **Hospitality suites.** The planner may be responsible for hospitality suites, which may be set up in a meeting room or in a guest room or suite.

The hospitality suite provides a place for participants to relax and to socialize with other participants. A bar is usually set up and hors d'oeuvres or light snacks are provided. (See Chapter 11.)

As explained, session management involves working with a number of different people before and during the meeting. Information has to be kept up-to-date, and as many details and policies as possible should be worked out before the meeting begins. Following are two session management checklists that can be used to monitor these details.

GENERAL SESSION MANAGEMENT CHECKLIST

Session Rooms	Location	Time	Rehearsal Time	Usage Before/After

❑ Adjunct rooms set up

❑ Entrance signs placed

❑ Session chairs briefed

INDIVIDUAL SESSION CHECKLIST

Session title _____

Room	Location	Time	Rehearsal Time	Usage Before/After

Session Chair _____

❑ Light controls located

❑ Temperature controls located

❑ Speaker handouts distributed

❑ Evaluation handouts distributed

❑ Entrance signs placed

Audience seating ❑ Classroom ❑ Theater Number _____

Refreshments provided ❑ Table service ❑ Station service

Number of pitchers/glasses _____

Table Materials ❑ List ❑ Distributed

Head table Location _____ Number _____

❑ Draped ❑ Flowers ❑ Signs

Podium ❑ Standalone ❑ Tabletop ❑ Center ❑ Sides

Lighting _____

See Audiovisual Checklist

Audiovisual Requirements

The type of meeting and the nature of the group that is meeting give a general indication of the meeting's audiovisual needs. For example, a corporate meeting for 20 board members might require a flip chart, marker board, and slide projector. The same corporation might hold a motivational meeting for its 300 sales representatives and use dozens of microphones, projectors, and screens. At many scientific meetings where technical papers are presented, slide and film projection is required for most of the speakers. The same might be true of a meeting of art historians, medical technologists, plumbing and heating contractors, or athletic coaches.

Audio needs at a meeting range from simple microphones to professional-quality stereo systems. Similarly, visual needs could range from a simple blackboard to an elaborate multiprojector videotape recorder and playback system.

Presentors should be encouraged to use audio and visual aids. During program planning, the Audiovisual Equipment Needs Forms (see Figure 4.1) should be sent to each presenter. Some presenters will bring their own equipment, but others may need assistance in operating unfamiliar equipment. The meeting planner should know in advance of each session who can handle equipment malfunctions and whether back-up equipment is available.

Sound Systems

Some kind of public address system is usually employed at meetings. Ideally, speakers who have an audience of more than 25 people should use microphones. In small meetings, the speaker might opt not to use a microphone if the audience can hear without it. More than one microphone might be needed at the head table for panel presentations. Microphones may also be placed at intervals throughout the audience to facilitate participation. The hotel usually charges for microphones and sets them up in the meeting rooms.

Microphones can either be attached to the podium or stand alone. Microphone stands can be adjusted to suit the speaker. Most microphones can be detached from their stands so that the speaker can walk around with it. A planner should check that the wires leading to the microphone have been taped to the floor so that no one trips over them. There are also very small microphones, called *lavalieres*, that can be pinned on a collar or hung on a cord around the speaker's neck.

Audio speakers and amplifiers are either built-in or portable. The built-ins are usually adequate for regular lectures and speeches, but more complex productions that feature music, for example, may require more power and better quality than a public address system.

If at all possible, audio speakers should be placed above the heads of the audience. A speaker that is placed on the floor directs sound to the knees of the people in the front row. Naturally those in the back don't hear as well, because the sound is absorbed by floor-level objects such as furniture, tablecloths, and legs. Placing microphones too close to speakers will usually produce the annoying squeal that is feedback.

Music adds atmosphere to many events. At low volumes, it can provide a nice background for receptions and banquets. Participants or presenters can dramatically march into a room to music. Patriotic songs may be played at opening sessions. Professional equipment will be required for most live performances, and most artists and entertainers will conduct their own sound checks. The meeting planner may be asked to reserve the performance room or hall for this purpose. The planner should work closely with the performer and the property to ensure that any hotel-supplied equipment or instrument works, that enough outlets are available, and that the performance room has good acoustics.

All public address equipment and musical instruments should be tested to confirm their reliability. Always test microphones and playback devices before each session. The bodies of the members of the audience will absorb sound, so if the test sounds too loud from the back of the room, volume is set correctly. During each session, there should be someone present (perhaps the session chair) who knows how to adjust the volume so that words and music can be enjoyed by the audience.

Visual Aids

Chalkboards, flip charts, and marker boards are examples of less sophisticated visual aids that individual speakers might use during their presentations. Overhead projectors may be used, although these are awkward to use and not as effective as slides. Electronic whiteboards can reproduce written material onto screens and photocopy the material onto paper. Supplies needed for these devices include chalk, markers, and transparency paper.

Slide projectors and film projectors are often used. Projectors may be operated either by a projectionist or by remote controls by the presentor. Some meeting rooms have projection booths behind the rear wall. For all projection equipment, be sure that extra bulbs are readily available.

Large spaces require high-powered projection equipment and a big screen. A small screen on a tripod will not project an image that can be seen by 200 people. Screens should be five feet above the floor to be seen over the heads of the audience. Many properties have permanent screens installed in meeting rooms. Another option is rear projection, in which the screen is placed in front of the projection equipment. Allow at last 20 feet behind the screen for rear projection. Sound should be connected to the house speakers. Be sure that the room can be sufficiently darkened for film projection, and always rehearse with projection equipment. If a portable screen is used, see if it can be draped for a more professional appearance.

One 19-inch VCR monitor is too small for viewing by more than 25 people, but several monitors can be spaced around the room. Some video equipment can project an image on a large screen. Note that videotapes that have been manufactured outside of North America may not be able to be played on standard VCR equipment.

An example of a very sophisticated visual aid is closed circuit television. It may be used when a speaker cannot actually attend a meeting. Many conventions use closed circuit television to feature brief addresses by nationally known figures, but arranging closed circuit transmission should not be left to amateurs. Closed circuit television can also be used to connect meeting participants electronically. Because of the costs involved and the careful coordination that is required, it is not feasible for all meetings.

As one would expect, computers have found their way into visual presentations. A speaker can now demonstrate a problem or compose a graphic image on a computer and project the image for the entire audience. This is particularly useful in training sessions. As mentioned, computers can also be used to enhance interaction between meeting participants or between meeting participants and speakers.

Specialized Services

At some meetings, it may be important to provide specialized assistance for speakers, participants, and people who cannot attend the meeting. The planner must see to it that the proper equipment, staff, and coordination is available to provide these services. Two such services are transcription and simultaneous language translation.

❑ **Transcription.** Many meetings are tape recorded in their entirety. The transcriptions of the meeting proceedings might be sent to those attending or perhaps sold to attendees and others. It may cost up to $300 per day to have a meeting professionally recorded and transcribed.

A commercial company may wish to get permission to audiotape or videotape a meeting and sell the tape. With these arrangements, there is no cost to the meeting sponsor. Within minutes of the end of a session, the tapes are available.

When videotaping, be sure that lighting does not distract the speakers. Lights should be placed well above speakers and not directed at their eyes. Speakers should also be encouraged to rehearse their presentations and wear clothing with colors and patterns that will be flattering to them on tape.

Last, be sure to get permission for audiotaping and videotaping. Typically, a release is signed in which it is made clear that the presentor understands that someone else will have the right to copy and distribute his or her material.

❑ **Simultaneous Language Translation.** An international meeting may require simultaneous language translation. The meeting room must have sufficient electrical capabilities for complicated wiring and translator space. Contractors and consultants can assist the meeting planner in this highly specialized field.

Another kind of simultaneous language translation is providing interpreters who translate the spoken word into American Sign Language (ASL) for hearing-impaired persons. The services of an ASL interpreter should be secured in advance of the meeting, and speakers should be advised that their presentations will be interpreted.

Costs

Audiovisual equipment and technicians can be quite expensive. In some localities, labor contracts control wages and set minimum labor charges.

Some properties have in-house audiovisual equipment and technicians, while others subcontract the work. Most properties will be able to provide microphones and screens.

Figure 10.6 shows sample audiovisual costs. While the planner will want to be sure that each presentor has what she or he needs, the planner should also be certain that what is ordered is actually used. It is not cost-effective to set up a slide projector in each function room if no one will be using the equipment.

Figure 10.7 shows the A/V needs and subsequent costs for a sample meeting. Costs for the transcriptions are also included.

Securing the right audiovisual equipment and finding competent technicians and operators can help the meeting planner avert having sessions that are plagued with problems. Using the audiovisual checklist that follows will remind the planner of the multiple tasks involved in this aspect of session management.

Equipment	Daily Rate	Equipment	Daily Rate
Video		*Meeting Aids*	
❏ ¾″ Cass. Player	$100	❏ IBM Typewriter	$50.00
❏ ½″ VHS Recorder	85	❏ Laser Pointer	50.00
❏ 19″ Color Monitor	85	❏ Flip Chart Easel	12.00
❏ 25″ RGB Color Monitor	125	❏ Flip Chart Pad	
❏ VHS Camcorder	200	(for purchase)	12.50
❏ Video Projector	Call for quote	❏ Flip Chart Marker	
		(for purchase)	2.00
Projectors			
❏ Overhead	$35	*Accessories*	
❏ 35 mm Slide	35	❏ 35 mm Wireless Remote Control	$20.00
❏ 16 mm Movie	40	❏ Projector Stand	10.00
		❏ 42″ Rolling Cart	15.00
Screens		❏ 54″ Rolling Cart	18.00
	Front Rear	❏ Extra Carousel Tray	2.50
❏ 6′ Tripod	$25 —		
❏ 8′ Tripod	35 —	*Labor*	
❏ 10′ Fast-Fold	70 $90	❏ Set-Up/Break-Down	$30 hr
❏ 12′ Fast-Fold	85 90	❏ Operator (3 Hr. Minimum)	$40 hr
Audio		*Labor Schedule*	
❏ Cass. Recorder	$40	7AM to 7PM Monday–Saturday Straight Time	
❏ Microphone	25	Over 8 hours of straight time	
❏ Lavalier Microphone	28	Time and a Half	
❏ Wireless Microphone	105	7PM to 12 midnight Monday–Saturday	
❏ 4 Channel Mixer	30	Time and a Half	
❏ Anchor Speaker	50	7AM to 12 Midnight Sunday	
❏ Sound Systems	Call for quote	Time and a Half	
		12 Midnight to 7AM Seven days a week	
		Double Time	
		Holidays	Double Time

Figure 10.6 **Sample Audiovisual Equipment Costs**

(logo)

ElecTech
123 Main Street
Anytown, USA
(100) 123–4567

To: C. Davison
234 First Street
Everytown, USA

Event _____   Location _____

Event dates/times: October 6–8, 19__

The following constitutes an offer of services and equipment for the above-named event, as per your requirements:

The ballroom is over 100 feet long and requires high-powered projectors.

	Per Day	*Total*
Zenon $200 (1st day); $100 subsequently		$400
2 12-inch lenses (each)	$25	150
1 10½ × 14 foot screen	65	195
1 set drapes	35	105
1 overhead projector	35	105
1 electric pointer	20	60
1 Caramate (slide previewer)	40	120
8 slide trays	no charge	
1 projectionist, 30 per hour (@ 28 hours) (4-hour setup and breakdown)		840
Equipment delivery & pickup		40
Recording and equipment	300	900
Transcription $3 per page @ 35 pgs. per hour (20 hrs)		2,100
TOTAL		$5,015

Please sign below and return.

_____   _____ __
ElecTech   C. Davison

Figure 10.7 Sample Audiovisual Equipment Contract

AUDIOVISUAL CHECKLIST

❏ Speakers queried as to needs
❏ Function sheets completed
❏ Hotel equipment confirmed
❏ Contract signed

Name _____

❏ Labor hired

Wages _____

Hours _____

❏ Transcription contracted

Name _____

❏ Transcription releases received
❏ Videotaping contracted

Name _____

❏ Videotaping releases received
❏ Translation contracted

Name _____

❏ Music contracted
❏ Session chairs given audiovisual requirements
❏ Ready room equipped

CHAPTER ACTIVITIES

1. Design a head table for a panel of six. Include decorations, microphones, and podiums.

2. Design a breakout session room for 20 participants and two speakers.

3. In your area, investigate the cost of renting:

    VCR

    VCR monitor

.High-powered slide projection equipment

Two spotlights

4. Contact a local hotel to see if it provides chalkboard, flip charts, and screens for meetings.

5. Find out what two different hotels charge to rent microphones.

AUDIOVISUAL SESSION CHECKLIST

Function _____ Location _____ Time _____

Session Chair _____

❑ Locate light switches

❑ Locate power sources

❑ Check window/door darkening

❑ Secure exposed wiring to floor

❑ Microphones   Number _____   Type _____

                  Placement _____ Speakers/amplifiers _____

    ❑ Test microphones

❑ Film projector   ❑ Screen

    ❑ Placement   ❑ Draping

    ❑ Extra bulbs   ❑ Test equipment

❑ Slide projector   ❑ Screen

    ❑ Placement   ❑ Draping

    ❑ Extra bulbs   ❑ Test equipment

    ❑ Remote control   ❑ No. of trays

❑ Overhead projector   ❑ Screen

    ❑ Placement   ❑ Draping

    ❑ Extra bulbs   ❑ Test equipment

    ❑ Transparency/markers

❑ VCR   Placement _____

    ❑ Monitors   Placement _____

    ❑ Cue tape   ❑ Test equipment

❏ Closed circuit TV   Placement _____

  ❏ Monitors   Placement _____

❏ Computer equipment   Placement _____

  ❏ Test equipment   ❏ Disks needed

❏ Tape recorder/CD player   ❏ Test equipment

  ❏ Tapes obtained

❏ Musical instruments   Placement _____

  ❏ Test equipment

❏ Flip chart   ❏ Paper/markers

❏ Chalkboard/whiteboard   ❏ Chalk/marker/eraser

Food and Beverage Service

Upon completion of this chapter, you will be able to:

1. Plan pleasing menus for meals
2. Arrange and coordinate receptions
3. Manage beverage cost and control
4. Budget F & B effectively

F ood and drink are not only essential for life, but are also sometimes the highlight of life. It is easy to appease our primary need for nutrition, but a well-planned and savory meal takes time to organize and prepare if it is to become an event. Meetings that only involve a food and beverage (F & B) function are common, but even if a meeting includes awarding honors, fund-raising, entertainment, hearing a speaker, and conducting business, the meal is often what commands attention.

If a meeting lasts more than three hours, some type of food and beverage, if only a snack, must be served. Sit-down meals, refreshment breaks, and receptions are customary components of meetings.

For each F & B function, the meeting planner will consider the following aspects:

1. Location—Where is the F & B function going to be held?
2. Timing—When is the F & B going to be presented?
3. Menu—What is going to be served?
4. Setup and service—What room setup or design is going to be used, and what type of service is going to be provided?
5. Cost—What is the F & B function going to cost, and how will access to the event be controlled?

Refreshment Breaks

Standing around the coffee machine or the soda dispenser is a classic office scene. The business day pivots on the traditional morning and afternoon break. Breaks are also an essential part of any meeting and are psychologically important to participants. Even if a meeting has no other F & B function, it will undoubtedly include a refreshment break.

Refreshment breaks are no longer limited to coffee and donuts. Coffee is still the mainstay of most breaks during a meeting, but a wider variety of food and beverages is being featured. Meeting properties are trying hard to satisfy today's health-conscious consumers, so it isn't surprising to see fruit, juice, bottled water, and low-fat, low-sugar baked goods on the refreshment table. Breaks might also include a short exercise program or an organized game to play.

❑ **Location.**   At some meetings, the coffee or refreshments are kept in the meeting room throughout the entire meeting day. (See Chapter 10.) The refreshment table is placed at the back of the room or along a side wall, and participants help themselves to refreshments. The property staff should be asked to restock beverages and snacks periodically.

At most meetings, however, refreshments are served in the vicinity of the meeting room. At large meetings, they are ideally set up near the registration/information desk and near rest rooms. Some properties have electrical outlets in the floor so that the refreshment service can be centered in an open space such as a foyer or lobby.

Holding the refreshment break in an entirely different place can turn it into something special. The pool, a terrace, or a penthouse are alternative locations. More time should be allowed for the break if it is to be held some distance from the meeting space.

❏ **Timing.** If formal refreshment breaks are established, the times are noted in the program or announced during the meeting. After two hours of sessions, a refreshment break should be scheduled to give participants the opportunity to move about.

Breaks are traditionally scheduled in the middle of the morning session and again in the middle of the afternoon session. For morning breaks, serving a bit earlier than the midpoint of the morning session is appreciated by people who do not eat a very hearty breakfast. Likewise, the afternoon break can be later; presumably, people have eaten sufficiently at lunch. Breaks should last from 20 to 30 minutes to give people time to obtain their refreshments, go to the rest room, make phone calls, and talk with other participants.

❏ **Menu.** Decaffeinated and regular coffee, tea, and possibly hot chocolate are standbys for a morning coffee break. Sweet rolls or Danish may be served, but sugar tends to slow people down, not boost their energy. Most hotels serve both coffee and soft drinks for an afternoon break. Sugar-free soft drinks and bottled water are popular beverage choices.

But these breaks are so dull! Creative planning livens up the traditional break. Yogurt, fresh fruit, raw vegetables and dip, trail mix, unsalted popcorn, and peanuts can be very tempting.

The menu for refreshment breaks can be built around a theme. With the hotel's assistance, the planner cold organize a "high tea" party complete with finger sandwiches and fine china cups. Or a carnival atmosphere can be created with balloons, popcorn, cotton candy, caramel apples, and servers dressed as clowns.

❏ **Setup/Service.** Refreshments are traditionally served buffet-style. In other words, participants help themselves to whatever they like. They open their own bottled drinks, pour their own coffee, and fill their own plates. Little assistance from the property staff is required, but most hotels add a gratuity to the cost of the break.

❏ **Cost/Control.** When ordering refreshments, estimate that everyone in attendance will drink one cup of coffee or one soda and will eat one of whatever food item is served. Some people will not have any refreshments, but others will have seconds. Note that the temperature of the meeting room can cause participants to consume more hot coffee or iced drinks than expected. The planner should regularly check to be sure that there are sufficient refreshments. Attendees can be irritable if they miss out on refreshments. Usually, the property staff can quickly replenish them.

The basic coffee and soft drink break is the least expensive, but do not be surprised if soft drinks cost $2 per bottle. The property charges by the can or bottle, keeping inventory of the number of items placed on the service table and the number that remain at the end of the break. Be sure to observe the size of the container and try to negotiate the price downward if it is the smaller six-ounce size. A 12-ounce size is usually opened, a glass filled, and the remainder shared with another person or left on the table for someone else. There is more waste with the larger size.

Hot drinks can be poured by a server and charged by the cup, but coffee is usually sold by the gallon in urns from which participants serve themselves. There are approximately 20 cups to a gallon, but this may vary depending on the size of the cup. Urns usually hold three or four gallons. A gallon of coffee may cost as much as $36.

Monitoring who is served at a coffee break that is held in a public area, such as the hall adjacent to the meeting room, is difficult. People from another meeting can walk up and help themselves to a cup of coffee or soft drink. There is little one can do about it except relax and realize that other meetings will also provide their own refreshment breaks, so losses will be slight. In enclosed or private areas, attendance control procedures (for example, tickets or name badges) can be enforced.

For low-budget meetings, attendees may be expected to pay by the cup or bottle for their own refreshments. More break time must be allowed to collect money and make change. If an honor system is employed, a sign and a container for money should be placed on the service table.

An outside organization may be interested in sponsoring a refreshment break. In return for such sponsorship, the outside organization receives publicity in the meeting program and may be allowed to display signs on the service table and distribute literature.

Refreshment breaks provide both a physical and psychological recess during meetings of all types. At some meetings, the refreshment break is the only time that participants can socialize.

Full-Course Meals

A perfect vichyssoise was followed by hearts of lettuce with marinated artichokes and a delicate vinaigrette. Then came the succulent, tender prime rib, small new potatoes smothered in real butter, and white asparagus. With each course, a vintage wine was proffered. A Sachertorte was the finale, served with a fine French brandy. Soft music, candlelight, flowers, crisp linen, sparkling crystal, china, and silver made the setting sublime.

We all remember certain meals. Though the food itself may not have been gourmet quality, the surroundings and ambiance were distinctive. When planning meals for meetings, the planner should try to ensure that they will be appreciated, if not memorable.

❑ **Location.** The vast majority of meals at meetings are served at the property at which the meeting is held. This is why it is so important to sample the food when choosing a property.

Meals should be held in rooms other than those in which the meeting sessions are being held. There might be a terrace or rooftop at the property where a meal would be appropriately served. Dinners or closing banquets at large meetings are often held in ballrooms.

Sometimes a meal is served in an exhibit hall or convention center. A caterer is usually hired to prepare and serve the meal, but otherwise meal management is the same as if the meal were served at the hotel property. If a meal is not part of the program, the exhibit hall or convention center might set up a sandwich bar or snack bar in its lobby.

It can be refreshing to leave the atmosphere of the meeting. However, planning for meals served away from the meeting site is complicated by the transportation needs of the participants. (See the section on dine-arounds below.)

❑ **Timing.** In North America, breakfast is usually taken between 7:00 and 9:00 A.M., lunch between 11:30 A.M. and 1:00 P.M., and dinner between 6:00 and 8:00 P.M. In Latin America and Southern Europe, the evening meal is not served until at least 9:00 P.M.

Meal times should be set when planning the meeting program. The number of diners in proportion to the number of servers affects dining time. Ordinarily 50 people can be served at a seated meal in one hour, but if the number of participants is greater than that, an hour and a half should be reserved for the meal. If a buffet breakfast is planned, schedule it for early birds and also for those that catch a last wink. If the meal accompanies the presentation of awards, a fashion show, or any ceremonial or entertainment event, the time allowed for it should be increased accordingly.

❑ **Menu.** The housemother at one university dormitory who was responsible for choosing dining hall menus was color-conscious. She liked to plan white meals, which consisted of chicken, rice, cauliflower, and potatoes. Her red meals included baked ham, beets, and pickled apple rings.

This woman needed help. A meal should not only be nutritious, but it should also be tasty and pleasing to the eye. Meeting planners work with the CSM, catering office, and chef to design menus and meal service. Most properties are willing to make suggestions and prepare food that are not listed on their main menus.

Menu planning is discussed in more detail below.

❑ **Setup/Service.** The setup time for a meal depends on the number of people to be served and can take 30 minutes for a 30-person meal or two to three hours for 300 people. If a meal is to be served in the same room as the meeting, be sure that prior to the meeting the tables are set with silverware, glasses, and china. It is almost impossible to set a table quietly.

The two basic styles of meal service are *seated service* and *buffet service.* At a seated meal, the food is brought to the diner, who is seated at a table. Seated meals require less time and are usually less expensive. At a buffet, diners serve themselves from a central serving table. A *scramble buffet* may be used where diners go to one station for salad, to another for the main course, and to another for dessert.

Figure 11.1 displays examples of buffet line patterns. Separate food lines should be established for every 75 people to be served. Half-rounds can be used to make curved corners, or serpentine-shaped buffet tables can combine for interesting effects.

For a buffet meal, tables may or may not be set for diners. If tables are set, then the planner must give the property staff instructions on what to place on the table. A buffet meal can proceed more efficiently if beverages, flatware, bread and butter, and condiments are already placed for each diner.

For sit-down meals (and for buffets where tables are available), ten square feet per person should be allowed. Probably the most common table shape is the round. A five-foot round will seat nine people maximum and a six-foot round will seat 10, though this does not leave much elbow room. Leave sufficient space between the rounds for servers and guests to walk. Rectangular tables are usually 30 inches wide and can be placed end to end if need be.

A complete dining room setup will often include space for a head table, buffet service tables, a dance floor, or an entertainment stage. Service styles are discussed in more detail below.

❑ **Cost/Control.** A sirloin steak, baked potato, tossed salad, brownie topped with ice cream, and half a bottle of wine would cost under $10 per person if prepared at home. The same menu can cost upwards of $50 per person for a banquet held in conjunction with a meeting. Meal costs are a big percentage of a meeting budget unless participants are eating "on their own."

Foods that have to be special ordered and shipped in are more expensive. Be aware of which foods are in season and try to plan the menu around them to cut costs. Wine adds to the cost of meals, and properties

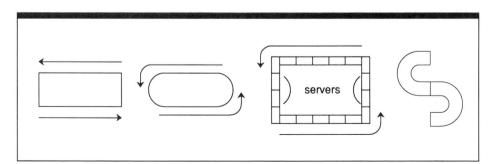

Figure 11.1 **Buffet Line Patterns**

mark up wine at a high percentage. Consider selling wine à la carte to lower F & B costs.

In addition to the cost of food and beverages, there are taxes and tips. Taxes vary by state, but average about five percent. Gratuities range from 15 to 18 percent.

Meal costs are usually figured on a per-person rate. Each meal prepared is called a *cover*, and charges are assessed for each cover. The planner must guarantee a certain number of people, which lets the property know how many people to expect for each meal. The property will require that this information be provided 24 to 48 hours before the event. If a banquet is guaranteed for 40 people, some properties charge for 40 meals even if only 35 people attend. At $50 per meal, the loss would be $250. For this reason, great care must be taken to get accurate counts of how many people will be served at each meal. Some properties give a five percent overage/underage on the guarantee. For example, if 40 meals were guaranteed, the property prepares for, can serve, and bills for 42 (five percent over 40). If attendance does not meet expectations, it charges for 38 and only 35 meals are served (five percent under 40).

Sign-up sheets can be posted at the registration desk for each meal. The planner can count how many people sign up for each meal and convey this information to the CSM. Meal tickets may be issued (usually in different colors for different meals). The planner keeps a tally of how many tickets have been given out or sold for each food function and gives this count to the CSM or catering department.

As with refreshment breaks, a sponsor might be found to underwrite the cost of a meal, a special beverage, or a dessert. Even in this case, it is still the meeting planner's responsibility to coordinate the menu and guarantees with the sponsoring organization, the CSM, or the catering department.

Service Styles

For seated meals there are four basic service styles:

❑ **Plate/American service.** Plates of food are prepared in the kitchen and placed before each diner.

❑ **Family/English service.** A waiter takes serving dishes of food to each table and gives it to a diner, who serves himself or herself. The platter is then passed from diner to diner.

❑ **Platter/Russian service.** A waiter brings serving dishes of food to each table and serves each diner.

❑ **Tableside/French.** The food is prepared by the food staff at the table and then served. For example, Caesar salad is often prepared tableside. Japanese restaurants also prepare many dishes tableside.

All four service styles have advantages and disadvantages. Family service is less labor-intensive, but judging the proportions that people will serve themselves is difficult. More time has to be allowed for platter and tableside service. With American service, one runs the risk of the food getting cold if the meal is not served on time.

The planner can consult any number of books on place settings. The number of courses to be offered indicates the amount of tableware. The formality of the meal determines whether placeplates (plates on which the salad plate or soup bowl is set and then removed before the main course) are used. The beverages to be served indicate which cups, saucers, glasses, and stems are set. Figure 11.2 shows a sample table setting.

Menu Planning

When selecting menus, the planner should keep the following criteria in mind. First, people are not only more conscious of nutrition these days, but they are also conscious of calories and the sources of calories. Gone are the meat and potatoes days. Good nutrition calls for balanced meals with proteins, starches, grains, and green and yellow vegetables.

Second, flavors should complement each other. Acid foods such as tomatoes and oranges are not compatible in one meal. Third, textures must be varied. Mashed potatoes and corn pudding are too similar to be served together. Fourth, colors should be varied. Green beans, broccoli, and asparagus will not be attractive if served during the same course. Finally, there should be a variety of foods and tastes. A mushroom salad should not be served with a meal in which the main course features a mushroom sauce. Similarly, a meal in which one kind of spiciness predominates will be boring.

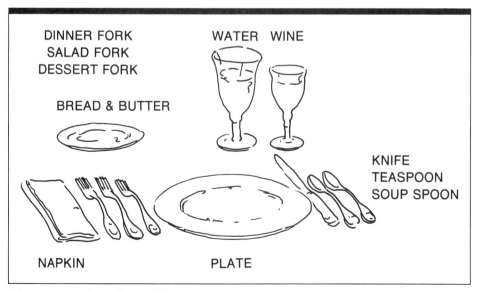

Figure 11.2 Sample Table Setting

Some people believe that food can affect moods, energy levels, and intellectual responsiveness. For example, many people feel drowsy after eating heavy meals. Therefore, lunches should have lighter menus than dinners. Figure 11.3 shows a sample luncheon menu.

The meeting planner should also remember that certain foods, such as shellfish, cause allergic reactions in many people. Also, some religions prohibit the consumption of foods such as pork. And more people are vegetarian. The meeting planner should try to find out if any of the meeting participants have special dietary requirements and then consult with the CSM or catering manager to meet the request.

Planning the menu includes choosing beverages. Juice, water, and hot coffee and tea are expected at breakfast. Iced tea is commonly served in the summer. Wine is often served with the evening meal, but state laws should be reviewed if spirits are to be served. In some states, no spirits can be served on Sundays or election day.

Most properties do not allow the meeting sponsor to provide its own alcoholic beverages because serving liquor is profitable for the property. If someone wishes to donate wine or champagne for an event, the planner should discuss it in advance with the CSM to see if an exception can be made. The property may still impose a corkage fee to open and serve the beverage, even if it is donated, or a gratuity on the estimated bottle cost, just as if the beverage had been provided by the property.

The wait staff can circulate pouring the wine for individuals, or the wine can be placed on the table with the diners serving themselves. For a table seating ten people, three bottles of wine will probably be consumed. Usually both white and red wines are served. If no wine is served with the meal, the wait staff can sell it by the bottle or glass to individuals who wish to pay for it.

Dine-Arounds

A dine-around can add a unique and entertaining experience to the meeting. Here the meeting planner reserves tables at a number of restaurants for a specific meal. The restaurants should be large enough to accommodate a few tables of meeting attendees. Ideally, the restaurants will all be of the same level of quality and cost and located fairly close to one another so that transportation time to and from each establishment is similar.

The meeting planner can estimate the number of tables to reserve from the number of registrants. It must be made clear to the restaurant that these numbers will be adjusted, but the planner should be precise about the time when reservations will be confirmed (usually, a minimum of 24 hours before the meal). It is virtually impossible to hold a dine-around on the first night of a meeting unless the number of meeting participants is known in advance and the meeting planner has already made reservations.

LUNCHEON MENUS

L-1
$17

Mixed White Crème de Menthe Fruit Cup
Cheese Straws
Mixed Endive-Romaine Lettuce
with Vinaigrette Dressing

Roast Loin of Veal
Blue Lake String Beans
Chateau Potatoes

Grand Marnier Cream
Petit Fours

L-2
$20

Port Angeles Smoked Salmon
with Vinaigrette
Mixed Spinach/Lettuce Salad
with Norwegian Blue Cheese

Champagne Sorbet

Prime Rib with Wild Mushroom Sauce
Asparagus á la George
Louisiana Wild Rice

Raspberry Crème
Dutch Chocolate Truffles

Meals include choice of beverage, coffee, tea (hot or iced), and rolls with butter.

All prices are subject to 5% sales tax and 18% gratuity.

Figure 11.3 **Sample Luncheon Menus**

If it has not been done in the preregistration process, attendees are given some kind of description and possible a menu from each participating restaurant at on-site registration. Sign-up sheets can be posted on which the attendees are asked to state their preferences. This information can be used to make reservations. If only a few people sign up for a particular restaurant, they might be persuaded to accept a second choice.

It is hard to out-guess attendees' culinary tastes. People tend to go with a group, and if two large groups choose the same restaurant, it might be sold out immediately. Throughout registration and restaurant sign-up, the planner should watch for over-booking at any particular property. A quick call to the restaurant might allow the planner the chance to revise earlier estimates.

Participants usually walk or take taxis, cars, or public transportation to the various restaurants. A meeting planner can organize bus or van transportation between the meeting property and the various restaurants if necessary. (See Chapter 12, which discusses transportation at the meeting.)

The timing of a dine-around should take into account whether another activity, event, or session follows. Sometimes restaurants are located at different distances from the meeting property. The service offered at each establishment will vary, thus the amount of time it takes to complete the meal will vary also.

Often dine arounds are paid for by those who eat at the individual restaurants. The planner merely makes the restaurant reservations. Participants usually order from the regular menu of the restaurant. It is possible, but a great deal of trouble, for the meeting planner to establish a set price for the meal with the restaurants. Here the cost is part of the meeting registration fee. A voucher is issued for the meal and presented at the restaurant. Each restaurant is paid for the number of meals that it serves.

If an equal price is set, each restaurant indicates what menu is available. This is a table d'hote (or table of the house) menu. Usually there is a choice of two or three main courses (probably a red meat and fish or chicken) and appetizers, salads, and desserts are included. When participants sign up for their restaurant choice, they might also choose their main course. The meeting planner conveys this information to the restaurant.

A dine-around may be an optional meeting event for which payment is made separately at the registration desk. Participants pay for their restaurant of choice (the cost may vary between restaurants) and are issued a voucher or ticket to present at the restaurant. The meeting planner settles the total bill later.

A variation of the dine-around is the pub crawl, where a variety of entertainment spots or bars are partially reserved for meeting attendees to visit. Often a shuttle bus has a central drop-off/pick-up spot that is near several suggested pubs. Attendees either pay for their own food and beverages or use vouchers that are good for a drink or a set dollar amount.

Dine-arounds take detailed planning and coordination and close counts and cost control. But the extra work usually results in added pleasure and good reviews from meeting participants.

Box Meals

Under certain circumstances, box meals can be the ultimate solution to a logistical problem. Most likely a box meal will be a box lunch. An imaginative and delicious box meal, eaten in an attractive setting, is no less appreciated than a sit-down meal.

❑ **Location.** Attendees are either given individually packed meals to eat where they please, or the meals may be distributed at a specific place, such as at poolside or on the golf course.

An example of when the box meal comes in handy is when a seminar is held at a college at which the dining facilities are filled to capacity during meal time. Participants can be given a box lunch and invited to eat on the college grounds. Box meals are also appropriate when the setting of the meeting is such that participants want time to enjoy the scenery. If the meeting participants are going on a sightseeing tour or field trip, a box lunch can be consumed en route.

❑ **Timing.** Another example of when the box meal comes in handy is when timing is very tight during the meeting. Eating on the run or in a bus is not particularly enjoyable, but may be necessary. On the other hand, eating a box lunch in a beautiful atmosphere can be very satisfying.

❑ **Menu.** Often the property where the meeting is held will make up the box meals and offer menu suggestions, or outside caterers can be engaged to prepare the box meals. Standard fare in a box lunch is a sandwich, chips, fruit, and cookies. Other choices include quiche, fried chicken, croissant or pocket sandwiches, potato salad or cole slaw, and unusual desserts. The point is to serve a balanced meal that can be consumed without making too much of a mess.

❑ **Setup/Service.** A box meal can be served anywhere. It can be distributed as participants file out of a meeting room or board a bus. It may be passed out upon arriving at a destination, such as a park or tourist attraction. The meeting planner should find out beforehand whether there are adequate refuse containers and whether there is any prohibition against consuming food and beverages at the meal site.

A box lunch can be presented in a variety of fashions: a brown paper bag; a plain white box; a decorative box or basket; or a giveaway tote bag. Whatever container is chosen should protect its contents and be able to be easily disposed of or carried for the balance of whatever other meeting activity is associated with the meal.

❑ **Cost/Control.** The cost of the box meal depends on its container and contents. The cost may be included in the registration fee or be optional. If charged separately, the cost may also be collected at registration; a voucher can then be given to the purchaser to be presented when the meal is distributed. A count must be given to the food preparation contractor.

The same principles regarding overage and underage apply to box meals as they do to other meals.

Receptions

A reception is basically a cocktail party. It may be a simple party at which guests are served one or two drinks, or it may be an affair at which enough drinks and food is served to qualify as a buffet dinner. Receptions easily lend themselves to themes.

❑ **Location.** A stage, a train car, and a paddleboat are examples of creative reception locations. A reception is generally more pleasant if held away from the meeting site. A new atmosphere promotes relaxation and conviviality.

The number of people expected to attend a reception determines the size of the space needed for it. At a stand-up reception, with no tables and chairs set up for guests, approximately nine square feet is needed per person.

❑ **Timing.** Receptions are traditionally held in the late afternoon or early evening between 5:00 and 7:30 P.M. They should be scheduled to begin after the last afternoon meeting session and to end early enough so that people have time for dinner. Often at meetings, there is a welcome reception, usually held the evening before the opening session. A reception may also be held before a banquet. It is certainly recommended that receptions serving alcoholic beverages be limited to two hours. It is also recommended that guests always have a nonalcoholic beverage choice, perhaps sparkling wine or soda.

Be sure to check with the CSM regarding when to schedule the reception. A property with unionized help may have to pay its house and wait staff time and a half for overtime after their regular hours.

❑ **Menu.** A full bar is stocked to serve a variety of mixed drinks. Sometimes guests have no choice of beverages—perhaps only wine, champagne, or bloody Marys are served. Theme receptions suggest food and beverage choices, such as Bahama Mamas being served at a Caribbean party. It is best to have several beverages on hand. Wine and soft drinks should be available. A reception can offer peanuts and potato chips or it can serve gourmet fare as shown in the sample menus in Figures 11.4 and 11.5.

When serving hors d'oeuvres or canapes, consider that each person will consume eight to ten items. Of course, certain well-liked foods, such as shrimp, will disappear before others. Most properties will be able to assist the planner with estimating how much food to order for the reception.

❑ **Setup/Service.** Guests can mix their own drinks or pour their own wine and sodas at a small, informal reception. At a more formal reception, one bar with two bartenders for every 75 to 100 guests is needed.

Our Chef Will Prepare On Site

TIDBIT STATION	***R-1***
Chicken Bits and Sirloin Tips (100 pieces)	$225.00
CRÊPE STATION	***R-2***
Paper-Thin Crêpes filled with choice of Creamed Chicken or Mixed Seafood (100 Pieces)	$275.00
PASTA STATION	***R-3***
Tortellini or Fettucini prepared with Alfredo and Mar- inara Sauce (Serves 100)	$300.00

All prices are subject to 5% sales tax and 18% gratuity.

Figure 11.4 **Sample Reception Menu (Per Event)**

Guests can order their beverages at the bar or waiters and waitresses can circulate through the crowd, taking orders and serving the drinks. Alternatively, pitchers with glasses or glasses that have already been filled can be set on a serving table. Guests can also either serve themselves from the buffet table or be served by the wait staff. Keep in mind that passing plates and cocktail forks is awkward. If food is served, it is far better to have several food stations instead of one large table. The buffet line patterns shown in Figure 11.1 can be adapted.

❑ **Cost/Control.** An organization might underwrite the cost of a reception. For important meetings, a CVB might host a reception to show off its convention center. A realtor might sponsor a reception at a new office building. A hospital seeking donations might sponsor a reception at its recreation center.

A reception can be paid for by the host organization or it can be a cash bar where guests buy their own drinks. Even for a no-host reception there is a charge for the bartender—this can be up to $40 per hour. A saucer for tips will also be placed on the bar. The property sets the price of anything sold at the bar.

Either the bartender takes cash for drinks, or drink tickets that are color-coded for specific drinks are sold. One or more ticket stations are set up with cash boxes. These ticket stations are staffed by property or meeting planning personnel. The planner must see to it that the sale of tickets is

RB-1

Fresh Vegetable Display
Beautifully Arranged with Dip Assortment

Mixed Seven Cheese Board Display
Served with Crispy Thin Sliced French Bread

Chesapeake Oysters and Clams on the Half-Shell

Mushroom Caps Stuffed with Maryland Crabmeat

$18.50 Per Person

RB-2

Succulent Tenderloin Roast Beef
Sliced to Order by our Chef
Served with Rye and Choice of Horseradish or Mustard Sauces

Virginia Cured Ham
Sliced to Order by our Chef
Served with Southern Biscuits and Jezebel Sauce

Elegant Fresh Fruit Display
Served with Honey Mustard and French Blue Cheese Dip

$22.50 Per Person

All prices are subject to 5% sales tax and 18% gratuity.

Figure 11.5 **Sample Reception Menu (Per Person)**

coordinated between the bartender and the ticket sellers. Guests may buy as many tickets as they want, or they may be given a limited number but be able to purchase additional tickets. The planner should purchase drink tickets for meeting staff who attend the reception.

For an open bar, guests order their beverages, which have already been paid for by the meeting organization or reception sponsor. The charge is determined by the drink, by the bottle, or by the person as stated in the meeting contract. If cost is assessed by the bottle, any opened bottle is charged to the account. Unfinished bottles should not (and cannot) be reused by the property. The planner should take them to use in the hospitality suite or wherever else seems appropriate.

In estimating cost, the average person consumes three drinks in the first hour, two drinks in the second hour, and one and one-half drinks in the third hour. The bartender can be told whether to serve one- or two-ounce drinks.

Well-prepared, attractively displayed, gracefully served food and beverages add greatly to the ambiance of a meeting. No matter what the meeting goals are nor how intense the sessions are, refreshment breaks, meals, and receptions provide the opportunity to make a pleasant memory. The Food and Beverage Service Checklist below can aid the planner in keeping track of these functions.

FOOD AND BEVERAGE SERVICE CHECKLIST

PLANNING

❏　1. Location _____

❏　2. Time _____

❏　3. Menu (including beverages) _____

　　　_____

　　　_____

　　　Special orders _____

　　　_____

❏　4. Number estimated _____

❏　5. Cost

　　　Per cover _____

　　　For service _____

　　　For reception food _____

❏　6. Theme _____

❏　7. Room setup _____

　　　Table size _____

　　　Buffet _____

　　　Head table _____

　　　Stage _____

　　　Dance floor _____

　　　Audiovisual equipment _____

Lighting _____

Color of linens _____

Bar available _____

❑ 8. Select service style _____

❑ 9. Attendance control procedure _____

    ❑ Print tickets

    ❑ Print sign-up lists

❑ 10. Plan program (entertainment/music) _____

❑ 11. Plan decorations _____

❑ 12. Request candles/flowers _____

❑ 13. Arrange head table seating _____

_____

❑ Escorts _____

_____

ON-SITE

❑ 1. Assign meeting staff duties

❑ 2. Admission control

    Describe _____

❑ 3. Give guarantee CSM

    Number _____

❑ 4. Consult with maitre d' regarding service

❑ 5. Install decorations

❑ 6. Check meeting room setup

❑ 7. Set tables correctly

❑ 8. Place flowers/candles

❑ 9. Place handouts

❑ 10. Check audiovisual equipment and lighting

❑ 11. Consult with speaker/entertainment/musicians—rehearsal

❑ 12. Count bar bottles

❑ 13. Sample food

On Your Own

At some meetings, attendees are expected to take care of their own meals. For example, a four-hour government seminar on purchasing regulations might allow a 15-minute break at 10 A.M. during which people go to coffee and snack machines for refreshments. No F & B service is involved. A five-day national convention could not be expected to hold 15 meals for all delegates, so people are expected to eat on their own, except for certain banquets or receptions.

If meeting participants will be eating on their own, the meeting property must have its own restaurants or be in the vicinity of restaurants. If people are expected to eat on their own for more than one day, they will appreciate having an assortment of restaurants to choose from. A property with its own restaurant or coffee shop should be prepared for crowds during the lunch break. The property may want to open a sandwich line near the meeting room to serve the participants.

In planning the program, the timing of the meal period must be extended if people are to eat on their own. A buffet or seated meal served at the meeting property can be concluded inside of an hour. If people are expected to locate a restaurant, place their orders, be served, and eat, it will naturally take more time.

Themes

Meals can be planned and enjoyed around themes. How is a theme chosen? The meeting itself may give the clue. A conference called "Exploring Foreign Markets" gives an obvious idea for a theme. An "Around the World" theme can use food and decorations from several countries. Perhaps three or four food stations at which the cuisines of different countries are featured will provide the meal.

Geographical regions suggest themes. A French, German, Mexican, or Chinese night can be successful. A country western night, a New England clambake, and a luau provide themes. Holidays—the Fourth of July, Halloween, or Bastille Day, for example—also suggest themes. Historical eras suggest themes. A 20s or 60s theme is always fun. Events supply ideas for themes. Carnivals, circuses, horseraces, and other sporting events present ideas.

Room decorations, menus, and costumes can easily reflect the theme. A particular color or print scheme can be used on the menus, tablecloths, napkins, flowers, and giveaways. Placecards with each diner's name can reflect the theme. Icing can be piped on desserts in symbols that show the theme.

A meal designed around a theme can be a huge production costing thousands of dollars more than an unadorned meal. A theme can also be conveyed with a small outlay of money for simple costumes, a few decorations, and several audiotapes.

CHAPTER ACTIVITIES

1. Plan a luncheon menu. Show how the following criteria are taken into consideration: nutrition; flavor; texture; color; and variety.

2. Estimate the cost of a two-hour reception for 150 people. It will be an open bar, and you are buying the drinks on a per-drink basis. Plan and price your reception buffet using the menus in this chapter.

12

Transportation and Free-Time Activities

Upon completion of this chapter, you will be able to:

1. Negotiate group rates with airlines
2. Understand how meeting planners and travel agents work together
3. Communicate with and organize travel for VIPs and presentors
4. Arrange charter transportation services
5. Organize recreation and entertainment events

A s with most of the other meeting planning activities, transportation and free time are both planning and on-site operations. Remember the instruction given at the outset: First read the entire book. Most of the activities discussed here should have been considered at the very first meeting planning session.

Transportation

It may be that the planner has no responsibility for meeting transportation. People can arrive on their own, and the entire meeting can be confined to one meeting property. On the other hand, the planner can be arranging transportation to the meeting for everyone, and there can be multiple sites to which participants must be transported for different meeting sessions. For example, people may be bussed to a convention center for an exhibit, a lecture held at a nearby university, or a free-time activity such as a live stage event.

To the Meeting

The availability and frequency of transportation is one of the major factors in picking the site for the meeting. The participant profile determines reasonable costs that people can be expected to pay to get to the meeting.

Automobiles

As noted earlier, participants at local meetings usually drive themselves to the meeting. Other participants may take taxis, buses, or subways. Organizations that hold county-wide or state-wide meetings also find that the majority of members arrive by private automobile. This situation poses few transportation problems for the planner. Everyone simply appears at the designated time.

People may, however, need assistance with parking. Motor inns, resorts, and airport hotels usually offer free parking, but free parking at center city locations seems to be a thing of the past. Spending ten dollars for all-day parking is not unusual in downtown locations.

It is nearly impossible to negotiate a favorable parking rate with a public garage, but it may be possible to negotiate the rate if the property owns its own lot or garage. For short luncheons or dinner meetings, there is little room to negotiate parking costs with the property, unless a great deal of money is being spent. The property simply charges a fee for every car parked, but the fee may be reduced.

The meeting sponsor may pay all or a portion of parking fees for attendees. Parking vouchers can be issued to meeting participants to give to parking attendants. Showing the meeting program to the parking attendant in order to obtain free or reduced parking rates is possible in limited circumstances. No-fee or reduced parking fees are viable marketing tools and should be mentioned in all meeting advertising and brochures.

Airlines

Airlines provide the chief means of transportation to many meetings. For larger meetings with a regional or national attendance, group air discounts can be negotiated with individual airlines. Obviously, an airline gains sales if it is known as the official airline or official carrier for a certain meeting. Although airline fares are very volatile, typical discounts are 40 percent off the standard fare or five percent off the lowest discounted fare available at the time of reservations. The trade-off for a low fare, though, is usually a penalty for making any change. The lowest fares are usually nonrefundable and must be purchased within strict time limits.

What are the benefits of discounted travel to a meeting? An airline contract typically includes a clause that for every 35 tickets sold to the meeting, the meeting organization receives one free ticket to destinations on that airline's routes. This can be used for transportation for the meeting planner and staff to the meeting site or to fly in presenters who live far away. The airline may also ship meeting materials to the site for free or at reduced rates and provide such conveniences as lists of attendees' arrival and departure times. Figure 12.1 shows a typical group air discount contract.

Which airline should be used? Obviously group rates should be negotiated with an airline that can serve the majority of your prospective participants. Usually, this is the airline with the most frequent service into the meeting city. A quick look at the *Official Airline Guide (OAG)* or a call to a travel agent can determine which airlines serve the meeting city from which geographical regions. Large cities usually have air service from a number of airlines, but often one airline dominates. The city in which an airline is headquartered usually has the most frequent service available. For example, Atlanta is the headquarters of Delta. Most people traveling to Atlanta will be able to fly in on Delta if they wish.

If a city is a hub for an airline, it will have flights from many different areas. For example, Baltimore is a hub city for USAir. At approximately the same time, flights take off from New York, Richmond, and Providence and land in Baltimore within the same time span. In Baltimore, the passengers from those flights can board USAir flights to other destinations.

Most airlines prefer to be the only vendor of group discount rates for a meeting. But if an airline cannot possibly serve passengers from east of the Mississippi, for example, then a second official airline can be chosen.

To obtain group discount rates for participants, there are two alternatives. A travel agency can work out the details or the planner can call the district sales manager of the airline directly. Travel agents get a ten percent commission on the sale of air travel. This is not an extra charge to the passenger, nor is it reflected in the fare. If the airline quotes $130 to fly between Pittsburgh and Washington, D.C., a travel agent will also quote

FLYAWAY AIRLINES, INC.
MEETING/INCENTIVE AGREEMENT

Flyaway is pleased to have been chosen the official airline for the

_____ meeting in _____

Contact _____

Title _____

Address _____

_____

Phone _____

Meeting Dates _____ Travel Dates _____

Flyaway Agrees to:

1. Make available Group Meeting Fares equal to the following percentages off: 45% off full coach fare with 14-day advance purchase and 40% off full coach fare with 7-day advance purchase.

The fares are valid from points in the contiguous 48 states to _____ airport(s). Should a lower Flyaway promotional fare be available, a 5% off lowest published fare with all restrictions being met will be offered.

2. Provide the Contractor one Flyaway ticket for travel on Flyaway for every 35 passengers who book the Group Meeting Fare and travel on Flyaway to the above-named meeting. These tickets may not be sold, bartered, or transferred and may be used only by the contractor's officers and employees.

3. Provide a meeting identification number and the use of the Flyaway Group Meeting Fare toll-free number (1-800-000-0000) for making reservations. These discounts are available only through this number.

4. Provide 1,000 flyers to the contractor concerning the Group Meeting Fare by June 1, 19-- .

The above-named contractor agrees to:

1. Designate Flyaway Airlines, Inc., as the official airline for the above-named meeting. No other carrier will be named such without Flyaway's written consent.

2. Promote the use of Flyaway's Group Meeting Fare in all promotional material. Copies of all promotional material must be approved by Flyaway prior to distribution.

3. The contractor indemnifies Flyaway against any loss of claim from the misuse of Flyaway's name.

This offer is valid until May 2, 19-- and becomes binding when signed by the contractor and by a Flyaway corporate headquarters representative. Flyaway shall not be liable for failure to perform under this contract because of cessation of service to an airport, accidents, strikes, acts of God, war, or governmental actions.

Accepted:
Flyaway   Contractor

_____   _____

_____   _____
Date   Date

Figure 12.1 **Sample Group Air Discount Contract**

the same price. An agent receives the commission from the airline for making the sale.

A travel agency that negotiates the group discount contract may wish to be designated the official travel agency for the meeting. A flyer can be included in the meeting registration packet that gives the agency phone number and the group discount number for reservations. Once the meeting participant's reservations have been made, either the official agency writes and mails the tickets or the participants use their own travel agents to make reservations and write tickets. Figure 12.2 shows a sample flyer that the official airline or agency may provide. This is also a valuable marketing tool for your meeting.

Because the airline and the agency keep excellent records, it is possible to track numbers and costs. Making payment by corporate credit card provides additional record keeping and protects the cardholder in the event of airline bankruptcy.

Meeting participants can also make their own arrangements by calling the phone number listed on the flyer, which connects them to the airline central meeting reservation center that handles group discount reservations. Quoting the number on the discount card enables the person making the reservation to pull up the meeting data.

The meeting planner is usually responsible for organizing travel for presenters, speakers, and other persons. Costs are harder to control if these people make their own travel arrangements and later ask for reimbursement. When the meeting planner or the official travel agency makes travel arrangements, the designated carrier is used whenever possible, which enables the organization to receive credit toward free tickets. Tickets can simply be mailed to these guests, or they can be prepaid (the guest picks them up at the airline office or at the check-in counter). The planner should

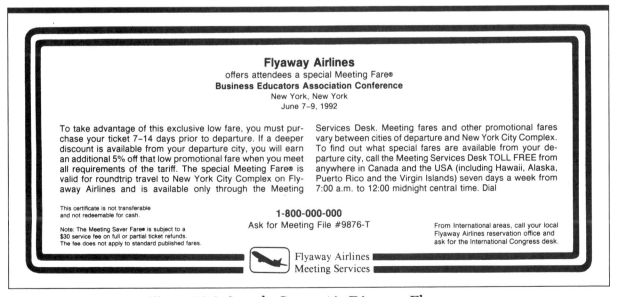

Flyaway Airlines
offers attendees a special Meeting Fare®
Business Educators Association Conference
New York, New York
June 7–9, 1992

To take advantage of this exclusive low fare, you must purchase your ticket 7–14 days prior to departure. If a deeper discount is available from your departure city, you will earn an additional 5% off that low promotional fare when you meet all requirements of the tariff. The special Meeting Fare® is valid for roundtrip travel to New York City Complex on Flyaway Airlines and is available only through the Meeting Services Desk. Meeting fares and other promotional fares vary between cities of departure and New York City Complex. To find out what special fares are available from your departure city, call the Meeting Services Desk TOLL FREE from anywhere in Canada and the USA (including Hawaii, Alaska, Puerto Rico and the Virgin Islands) seven days a week from 7:00 a.m. to 12:00 midnight central time. Dial

This certificate is not transferable and not redeemable for cash.

Note: The Meeting Saver Fare® is subject to a $30 service fee on full or partial ticket refunds. The fee does not apply to standard published fares.

1-800-000-000
Ask for Meeting File #9876-T

From International areas, call your local Flyaway Airlines reservation office and ask for the International Congress desk.

Flyaway Airlines
Meeting Services

Figure 12.2 Sample Group Air Discount Flyer

be careful when sending tickets through the mail. Depending on timing, tickets may have to be sent by overnight mail; the planner should take this cost into account. A $900 ticket should not be sent overseas through regular mail.

Figure 12.3 shows a sample form that can be sent to presentors to find out how they wish to travel to and from the meeting. This should be sent to them at least two months before the meeting. This is also an opportune time to send travel policies and travel claim forms to be used by presentors when requesting reimbursement. The meeting sponsor should make it clear what documents should be attached and when reimbursement can be expected. People who are traveling from overseas may want to be reimbursed immediately in U.S. dollars. Figure 12.4 is a typical expense reimbursement form.

The least expensive airline tickets have many rules and restrictions. Staying over a Saturday night usually lowers round-trip airfare, but few meetings are held over weekends. Actual restrictions vary, but airlines may require that tickets be purchased 14 days in advance, for example. In addition, the ticket may be nonrefundable and the traveler may not be permitted to make changes without paying a steep penalty.

There is a fine line between the benefits of realizing savings by purchasing lower-priced nonrefundable tickets and purchasing full-fare refundable tickets. A presentor with a busy schedule may have to change his or her flight arrangements, which will cause heavy penalties if a discounted restricted ticket has been purchased. If nonrefundable tickets are purchased, any restrictions on the ticket should be made clear to the recipients. If changes are needed, it might be agreed that the person is responsible for any penalties. Because this can be awkward, many meeting sponsors opt to purchase refundable tickets at the higher price.

Another foil in dealing with travel arrangements is frequent flyer woes. Some people plan their flights in order to accrue frequent flyer miles. Presentors sometimes insist on a particular airline, but if a group discount fare has been arranged and the number of flights taken by meeting participants confers benefits on the meeting sponsor, then presentors should not be given a choice of airlines. If the designated carrier does not provide adequate service for the presentor, however, the meeting planner should try to abide by the presentor's wishes.

During the Meeting

Once the meeting participants have gotten to the city in or the property at which the meeting is being held, ground transportation (or transfers) may still be needed. The planner usually must arrange for this transportation or at least inform participants of what is available.

Environment Association Conference
Eastern Europe Tomorrow

June 7, 8, 9, 19XX

King Plaza Manhattan, 600 Duke Street, New York NY 10019, (212) 000-0000

REQUEST FOR TRAVEL ARRANGEMENTS

Name _____

Title _____

Affiliation _____

Address _____

City/State/ZIP _____

Work Phone (__)_____ Work Fax (__)_____ Home Phone (__)_____

TRANSPORTATION

Air _____ Rail _____ Personal Auto _____

Departure from (City) _____ Airport/Station _____

Departure Day/Date _____ Desired Time _____

Arrive in New York _____

Departure from New York Day/Date _____ Desired Time _____

ACCOMMODATIONS: KING PLAZA MANHATTAN

Arrival date _____ Single _____

Departure date _____ Double _____

Special requirements _____

Please complete and return to Mr. Hampton, The Environment Association, 1234 Fifth St., Washington, DC 20000.

Tickets and confirmed reservation vouchers will be provided 10 days prior to your desired arrival date. For information and change in plans contact Mr. Hampton at (202) 000-0000 or (202) 000-0001 (**FAX**).

Figure 12.3 Request for Travel Arrangements

TRAVEL EXPENDITURE STATEMENT
(PLEASE READ INSTRUCTIONS ON REVERSE SIDE)   No._____

Name _____ Date _____ 19 ____

Date of Departure _____ Date of Return _____ No. of Days _____

Cities Visited and Purpose of Trip _____

Expenses:	Dates								Total Cost of Trip	Payments Made Directly by Company	Cash Expended
(A) Plane											
(A) R.R. inc. Pullman											
(A) Bus											
(B) _____											
(C) Lodging											
(D) Meals											
(E) Taxi, etc.											
(F) Registration Fee											
(G) Entertainment											
(H) Miscellaneous											
(I) _____											
							Total				

Please Indicate the Amount of Personal Expenses to be Repaid _____
°Payments made directly by Company through advance payments or credit cards

Cash Advanced _____
Difference due:
   Company   _____
   Employee   _____
Organ. No.   _____

Pay to   Amount   Ticket No. or Voucher No.   Credit Card No.

Entertainment:

Date _____ Place (Name of restaurant, etc.) _____

Type of Entertainment _____

Amount: Meals _____Other (Explain) _____

Names and business relationship of persons entertained _____

Business, Purpose, Nature of Business Discussion, and Expected Benefit (Not Needed For Business Meals) _____

Remarks: _____

For Accounting Dept. Use Only	For Cashier's Use Only

Amount of Payment $ _____

Organ. Code	Charge Number	Amount

Non-Taxable—(5) _____

Examined & Cal. Verified _____

Dispatched _____ Approved _____

RECEIVED OF _____ CASHIER,
$ _____ BEING TOTAL OF PERSONAL
FUNDS USED IN EXCESS OF AMOUNT ADVANCED
SIGNED _____

Employee Signature _____

Approved _____

It is important that supporting vouchers such as receipted hotel bills, transportation stubs, etc., be attached to this claim.

Figure 12.4 **Expense Reimbursement Form**

Rental Cars

Just as airlines do, rental car companies are often willing to negotiate group discounts for meeting attendees. Many attendees prefer to have a car available during a meeting. Advertising flyers with 1-800 reservation numbers and the group discount code should be included in registration packets.

For incentive meetings, rental cars may be reserved and paid for by the meeting organization for each participant. However, in doing so, the organization exposes itself to liability in the event of an accident. One way to minimize this risk is to use vans seating six to eight passengers and to use company-paid drivers.

Some incentive meetings include transportation by chauffeur-driven limousine. More and more of these block-long, elegant automobiles are seen at airports, where uniformed drivers hold up signs with their passengers' names in the arrival area. Limousines can be hired for the duration of the meeting, delivering their very contented passengers to different sites.

Public Transportation

For those who do not drive to the meeting or who are not driven to the meeting site, public transportation between airports, bus terminals, and train stations and the hotel must be considered. Meeting participants may be expected to use taxis, buses, subways, or airport shuttle services.

It is a courtesy to include city maps in the meeting registration packet, and if the planner expects more than 50 people to attend the meeting, the planner should notify taxi and shuttle bus companies to expect additional business. The planner may consider stationing a person who can welcome attendees at the airport and direct them to transportation.

These local transportation costs may be solely the responsibility of individual participants or they may be included in the participant's registration fee. If included, vouchers, coupons, or tickets are sent to each participant. The planner contracts with the transportation companies to accept the vouchers and pays the carrier when presented with the collected tickets.

Many properties have courtesy vans that shuttle guests between the hotel from the airport. In large cities, there is usually a public limousine or motorcoach service that has a set route from the airport throughout the city, stopping at strategic hotels, the convention centers, and sometimes shopping centers or bus terminals in the suburbs.

The following checklist can be used to record ground transportation requirements.

GROUND TRANSPORTATION CHECKLIST

Number and names of rental car companies _____

Negotiated discounts _____ Promotional material _____

Group van rental _____ Designated drivers _____

Limo service _____

Public transportation

❑ Airport bus

❑ Subway

❑ City bus

❑ Taxi

❑ Hotel van

❑ Participants sent information/maps

❑ Companies notified of meeting

Chartered motorcoach

Paid by ❑ Participants ❑ Meeting ❑ Hotel

Estimated usage _____

Equipment _____

❑ Participants notified

Motorcoach Transportation

Chartering buses may be the solution to transporting meeting participants. This may be for airport to hotel transfers, between meeting properties or for off-site sessions or events.

Transfers

Rather than have participants make their own travel arrangements, the meeting planner or property can rent buses or vans for transportation between terminals and hotel. The contract negotiated with the property may include provisions for the property to handle these arrangements and payments. If not, the planner charters transportation, negotiating, contracting, scheduling, and paying for transfers.

If the official carrier or travel agent provides a list of participants' arrival and departure times, the planner or the meeting property can coordinate when to have ground transportation available at the airport, terminal, or depot. The average bus accommodates 50 people, and vans seat six to ten passengers.

Participants should be told when transportation will be available so that they can schedule their arrivals in conjunction with that schedule. A ground transportation schedule can be included in the registration packet.

At registration or sometime during the meeting, participants can sign up for return transportation at a specific time.

Shuttle Services

For large meetings at which attendees stay at several different hotels, transportation must be managed with precision. Participants need transportation to the convention center, to the headquarters hotel, between hotels, and to sessions or events in locations other than the headquarters hotel. The planner can rent motorcoaches to shuttle between major hotels and the convention center. First, the route between hotels should be plotted. It may be necessary to contact the city police to confirm that the motorcoach routes are permitted. Hotels or other sites where stops will be made must be asked about parking regulations, overhangs, and the spaciousness of their driveways.

The overall meeting program should guide the shuttle schedule. For example, the shuttle busses might stop first at those hotels that are hosting the most meeting participants. This allows the greater percentage of attendee-passengers to board first. If it appears that more buses will be needed at later stops than were planned, the motorcoach operator can be called sooner rather than later. Allow for rush hour traffic and inclement weather. The number of buses needed will vary for different times of day, according to sessions scheduled. The meeting planning staff should monitor how the buses are operating and whether more or fewer buses would be adequate.

Other than providing continuous shuttle services, the meeting planner might have to also arrange for transportation to select sites for particular activities. For example, the Convention and Visitors Bureau may sponsor a reception to show off its new visitor's center. The meeting participants need to be brought to the center at 6 P.M. and returned at 8 P.M. Or perhaps a motorcoach will be hired to drop participants off at restaurants for a dine-around. For large meetings, the planner and motorcoach operator might have to work out a schedule to pick up participants from several locations.

The meeting program should state whether transportation will be provided to sessions and events that are taking place away from the meeting property. If people are expected to gather in the lobby of a hotel at a certain time to board a bus, that should be noted as well. Allow plenty of time for people to go to their rooms to freshen up or change clothes or shoes before going off site.

Contracting Transportation

When the meeting is being planned, motorcoach operators should be contacted to make bids for the charter services required. Some school districts own buses that are available (particularly in the summer), but generally the planner will work with private operators.

The cost for chartered transportation includes several components. First, there is usually an hourly cost for the vehicle and its driver. The bid might include transportation time for the buses to get to the site from the garage. A minimum number of hours may be required per vehicle. The planner should understand whether the minimum time has to be used in one block or whether it can be split (that is, three hours in the morning and three in the afternoon). Additional vehicles and drivers will likely cost more. Sometimes vehicles that are dispatched but not needed cannot be returned in order to save money.

Price is not the only consideration in choosing the motorcoach operator. Does the operator have enough vehicles to handle the job? Does it have past experience with the type service needed? Can references be provided? Are insurance records impeccable? Are licenses up-to-date? Are the vehicle seats comfortable and in the needed configuration? Does the vehicle have adequate ventilation, air conditioning, and heating? Is there a rear door to speed up loading and unloading? Is there an on-board restroom? On-board food facilities? Is there a hydraulic lift for handicapped people? Is the vehicle radio dispatched? When using several coaches, can the drivers communicate with each other?

Buses must be clearly marked for the meeting. Signs on the front, back, and sides of the motorcoach should give the meeting name and, if needed, route information. Signs should also be placed at stops and loading zones.

Drivers should have exact directions and be provided with maps of their routes. If drivers are expected to collect payment for transportation, instructions and policies should be given to them in writing. Emergency procedures to cover mechanical failure, health emergencies, bad weather, or extreme delay should be established.

A checklist to use when chartering a motorcoach is shown below.

MOTORCOACH CHARTER CHECKLIST

Dates needed _____

Pick up point(s) _____ Drop off point(s) _____

Schedule times:

　　　Pick up _____ Drop off _____

　　　Pick up _____ Drop off _____

　　　Pick up _____ Drop off _____

Maximum number using _____ Minimum number using _____

Equipment needed _____

_____

Payment arrangements _____

Signs _____

Information distributed _____

CONTRACT CONSIDERATIONS

When evaluating bids from several companies, rank the following items on a numerical scale. 5 = Excellent, 4 = Good, 3 = Average, 2 = Below Average, 1 = Poor.

Equipment:

Clean ____	Good repair ____
Seats comfortable ____	Configuration ____
Ventilation ____	Air conditioning/heat ____
Restroom ____	Food service area ____
Handicapped accessible ____	Loud speaker ____
Radio dispatched ____	Storage space ____

Company:

References ____	Experience ____
Licensed ____	Insurance ____

Emergency/break down arrangements _____

_____

Cost:

Per hour _____   Per person _____

Travel time to/from garage included? ❑ Yes ❑ No

Minimum hours? ❑ Yes ❑ No Number _____

Can minimum be split? ❑ Yes ❑ No

Can equipment be added? ❑ Yes ❑ No Additional cost? _____

Can equipment be returned unused? ❑ Yes ❑ No

   Additional cost? _____

Free-Time Activities

Every meeting should schedule some free time—time away from meeting sessions. How this free time is spent can be left up to the participants or can include planned events. Incentive meetings consist almost exclusively of free time.

Free time is generally spent on three activities: entertainment, recreation, and sightseeing. These may overlap. At meetings, free-time activity can also include programs for adults and children who accompany the meting participant as well as programs that are held before and after the formal meeting program.

Planning free-time activities does not mean just ordering tickets for the ballet and telling people when to arrive at the theater. A meal might be part of a free-time activity, and transportation may have to be arranged for people to take advantage of the activity.

Entertainment

Entertainment may be scheduled as part of the meeting program and held on-site. It can be a professional Broadway-type show with exotic costumes, lighting, and sound effects. On a simpler scale, a talent contest among meeting participants is a popular entertainment option. Local singing groups or little theater companies may be engaged to provide entertainment during a meeting.

Meeting participants can also be taken to entertainment events that are occurring in the meeting city. Concerts, sports, plays, and choral productions are but a few of the many opportunities. For some groups, the meeting planner might be able to set up a "meet the stars" reception on stage following a performance or arrange autograph sessions.

Participating in a free-time activity may be optional. Individuals sign up for the event, pay for it, and then receive their tickets. Sometimes the cost of special entertainment is included in the registration cost. For optional events, the planner should try to block seats, which are then available for sale until a certain time. If the planner has to purchase the tickets, there is a chance some will not be sold, which incurs a loss.

Recreation

The mere presence of a swimming pool or recreation room at a property provides opportunities for free-time activity. Many hotels now have gyms with exercise equipment available free or for a small charge.

Golf and tennis are probably the most popular recreational activities. With the help of the tennis or golf pro, the meeting planner can organize tournaments between players, setting up flights, scheduling playing times, and giving awards. Trophies or other prizes can be given at the final meeting dinner or banquet.

Oceanside properties provide opportunities for snorkeling, windsurfing, and waterskiing. Beachfront volleyball tournaments and even limbo contests provide healthy recreation.

Again, recreational activities can be paid for by the people who enjoy them, or their costs can be included in the registration fee. Costs of greens or court fees, rental equipment, professional administration, and trophies must be considered if such activities are included in the registration costs.

Sightseeing

Probably the most common free-time activity during meetings is sightseeing, although visiting tourist attractions does not appeal to everyone. Most larger cities have tour operators who are more than willing to arrange sightseeing for meeting participants. The cost of sightseeing can be paid for out-of-pocket by participants or it can be included in the cost of registration.

If sightseeing is an "on-your-own" activity, brochures and information on available tours can be displayed at the meeting registration area. A tour company may want to have its sales staff at the registration area to sign up customers.

If the meeting organization is paying for the tour, the number of sightseers must be determined. This can be done before the meeting when making meeting reservations or upon registration. The count must be accurate because it indicates how many motorcoaches and guides are needed.

Companion Programs

More and more people who attend meetings are accompanied by companions. If the participant profile indicates that a great many spouses or significant others will be at the meeting site but not registered to attend the sessions, then some activities should be organized for them.

Companions might enjoy entertainment, recreation, or sightseeing, or other events can be scheduled. In the past, fashion shows, crafts demonstrations, and shopping tours were standard for women who accompanied their husbands to meetings. With today's mixed work force, creativity is needed to orchestrate a successful companion program.

Abbreviated seminars on the subjects being discussed at the meeting make for better conversation between participants and their companions. For example, perhaps those accompanying participants at a computer convention would like to know something about the software that is being introduced during the meeting. Or a speaker on personal finance may interest a stockbroker's companions.

Some cities have companies that specialize in planning companion programs. The CVB should have this information. Local members of the meeting organization may have ideas; their own companions may want to entertain the visiting companions.

Companion programs may be paid for individually. With incentive meetings, the costs are often covered by the meeting organization. Descriptive flyers about companion activities should be included in the registration packet. Prior sign-up should be required because any speakers or contractors will have to be confirmed.

Children's Programs

If the participant profile indicates that children may accompany their parents to a meeting, the planner might want to prepare a list of child care services for participants. Be sure that the day care centers are licensed and insured before listing them on any meeting material. Indicate the source of the information on the list (for example, the CVB) and include a disclaimer that the meeting management is not recommending any specific child care facility.

Certain meetings provide child care during meetings. This can be complicated, expensive, and time-consuming for the planner. Cots, cribs, sleeping mats, food, water, bathrooms, play equipment and highly trained personnel must be provided. Often a registered nurse is required. Health and food regulations are often stringent for temporary child care facilities.

Children may be taken on their own sightseeing tours or games, and contests may be organized to entertain them. The ages of the children involved will suggest some activities and rule out others.

Pre-Meeting and Post-Meeting Tours

At additional cost, people may take advantage of tours before or after a meeting. These may be day trips or longer excursions. For example, a three-day cruise following a meeting in Miami would probably be very marketable.

A travel agent or tour operator will usually handle all of the details of the tour, including marketing. The meeting planner's responsibility is to check the tour operator's references very closely. The planner should provide the organizer with a profile of the meeting group and advise on appropriate itineraries. Ideally, the tour will involve only meeting participants and their companions and give them benefits not ordinarily offered to the general public.

For most meetings, the planner becomes involved in transportation even if it is no more complicated than transporting staff to the meeting site, yet for many meetings transportation is a complex part of planning. Transportation and free time management are tied closely together. Providing free time during meetings is essential. Organizing free-time activities for a group can be complicated but can also make the difference between an outstanding and a merely adequate meeting.

CHAPTER ACTIVITIES

12

1. Contact a motorcoach company to find out its rates and restrictions.

2. Determine the ground transportation services at your nearest airport.

3. Talk to a travel agent about the services available through the agency for meeting support.

4. Name five local entertainment groups that might be available to perform at a conference in your city.

5. Write down four entertainment and recreation possibilities available in your area.

6. Investigate sightseeing opportunities in your area.

Evaluation and Follow-up

Upon completion of this chapter, you will be able to:

1. Judge what to evaluate

2. Determine what method of evaluation to use

3. Complete follow-up activities efficiently

G etting a grade on a report card is something students either dread or anticipate confidently. A good report card is an appraisal that can be the basis for positive change. Likewise, evaluating a meeting must be done with the same kind of care and professionalism that the meeting planner brings to every other aspect of meeting management.

To evaluate means to determine the worth of, and information from evaluations is important for the planner and the organization. Were the meeting objectives met? Was the meeting worth the effort? Even if a meeting is held simply for pleasure, whether or not the enjoyment of its attendees was worth the trouble of its organizers must be judged.

Meetings designed primarily to produce income have a simple success/failure criterion: money was either made or lost. Incentive meetings are very expensive, and whether or not they achieve their goal (usually to increase sales performance) is important. This can be determined by subsequent sales figures and the number of participants that qualify to attend the next incentive meeting.

Methods of Evaluation

Evaluations can be conducted in several ways. People can be appointed to attend certain general and breakout sessions and asked specific questions about them. These may be people who hold offices in the meeting organization or who have been presentors in the past, or they can be arbitrarily chosen from the general meeting audience. Another evaluation method is to interview participants randomly for their opinions. Evaluations can be done during the meeting or at the end of the meeting, or after the meeting. It can be more expensive to mail evaluations to people after the meeting, however, and the return rate can be lower.

Even when other evaluation methods are used, management should gather to brainstorm and review evaluation statistics.

Evaluation most commonly takes the form of questionnaires that meeting attendants are requested to complete. Most people are flattered to be asked their opinion and are more than willing to fill out a questionnaire. The easiest form of evaluation is ranking or rating different criteria on a numerical scale. In most cases, the rankings of 5 for excellent, 4 for good, 3 for average, 2 for below average, and 1 for poor will do. Any special evaluation instructions should be carefully explained.

There is a great deal of computer software available to compile information gleaned from questionnaires. Optical scanners can also convert simple pencil marks into useful statistics.

As with most things, conducting even the most rudimentary evaluation has a cost in terms of time and money. Materials may have to be printed, computer time might have to be scheduled, and several people might have to take time to interpret the evaluation.

Questionnaires can be placed on seats before a session and collected by the session chair at the conclusion of the session. To get people to complete a general meeting evaluation, a small gift may be offered when a form is turned in. This may be as simple as a writing tablet. When evaluations are vital, something of greater value may be given to those who turn in the questionnaire. A simple contest (name the newsletter, complete the puzzle) or a drawing for a prize also motivate people to fill out a form.

Criteria for Evaluation

Most of the meeting's components—that is, the geographical site, the specific property, the sessions, and the overall meeting—should be evaluated after the meeting. The meeting property may have been perfect when the planner inspected it, but how did the meeting participants like it? Was the timing and pace of sessions appropriate for the topics under discussion, or did participants complain about feeling rushed? The keynote speaker came highly recommended and looked wonderful on a video clip, but was the message understood and appreciated by those who heard it?

It may be too time-consuming and expensive to survey absolutely everything about a meeting, but the planner should be able to find out generally what worked and what didn't.

❏ **Site.** The geographical site and its amenities should be appraised. Future desirable locations can be discovered by asking specific questions about the nightlife, friendliness, safety, and beauty of the city or area in which the meeting was held. Indications of whether participants would prefer a city or a resort in the future becomes clear.

GEOGRAPHICAL SITE EVALUATION

On a 1 to 5 scale, rank the following about city name. 5 = Excellent, 4 = Good, 3 = Average, 2 = Below Average, 1 = Poor.

_____ Convenience of transportation from my hometown

_____ Entertainment

_____ Sightseeing

_____ Restaurants

_____ Shopping

_____ Recreation

_____ Friendliness of residents

_____ Cost of living

_____ Total Score

What geographical area do you suggest be considered for a future meeting?

_____

Comments _____

_____

_____

❑ **Property.** The property in general as well as its meeting rooms, sleeping rooms, food, service, and facilities should be evaluated. The planner needs guidance for choosing properties in the future for the participants of a particular meeting. Most properties welcome evaluations, and many have their own questionnaires. The Site Selection Checklist in Chapter 5 provides many of the questions.

Rating a property brings interesting things to light. One group may not care that there is a swimming pool. Another group may indicate that they expect a higher level of service at a property.

When evaluating the property, food and beverage both at meeting sessions and in public dining areas should be rated. The planner may be able to deduce trends, such as that the majority of a meeting group dislikes fish or that no one eats in the hotel restaurant, that will modify future site selections.

PROPERTY EVALUATION

On a 1 to 5 scale, rank the following about the city in which the meeting was held. 5 = Excellent, 4 = Good, 3 = Average, 2 = Below Average, 1 = Poor.

_____ Location

_____ Transportation availability

_____ Price

_____ Luxury level

_____ Public restaurants

_____ Meeting food and beverage service

_____ Check in/out

_____ Recreation

_____ Exhibit space

Meeting rooms

_____ Location

_____ Decor

_____ Floor plan

_____ Furniture comfort

_____ Temperature comfort

_____ Acoustics

_____ Lighting

Sleeping rooms

_____ Decor

_____ Cleanliness

_____ Ventilation/lighting

_____ Security

Service

_____ Efficiency

_____ Front desk

_____ Uniformed personnel

_____ Food servers

_____ Room service

_____ Shops/office support: (list)

_____ Total Score

Comments _____

_____

_____

❑ **Overall Meeting.** Next, the meeting in its entirety must be evaluated. This includes program content and the organization and management of the meeting. Whether the meeting's objectives were achieved needs to be determined. Was timing of the meeting good? Would the participant attend a similar meeting next year? Which were the most and least valuable sessions?

GENERAL MEETING EVALUATION

On a 1 to 5 scale, rank the following about the meeting. 5 = Excellent, 4 = Good, 3 = Average, 2 = Below Average, 1 = Poor.

_____ Meeting objectives defined and met

_____ Time of year meeting held

_____ Length of the meeting

_____ Days of the week

_____ Cost

_____ Geographical location

_____ Property

_____ Transportation

_____ Usefulness to me

_____ Time spent was

_____ General sessions

_____ Breakout sessions

_____ Speakers in general

_____ Exhibit

Food/beverages

     _____ Meals

     _____ Coffee breaks

     _____ Receptions

_____ Free-time activities

Marketing materials

     _____ Announcements

     _____ Advertising

     _____ Direct mail

          _____ Appearance

          _____ Timeliness

_____ Mail registration processing

_____ On-site registration processing

Meeting materials

     _____ Program

     _____ Attendee list

    ____ Exhibitor list

    ____ Nametags

    ____ Other

____ Information desk service

____ Meeting signs

____ Total Score

Suggestions for next year _____

_____

_____

Comments _____

_____

_____

❑ **Sessions.** As mentioned before, each session can be evaluated. This is best done at the end of sessions with the session chair collecting the evaluations. Information from this evaluation will help choose future speakers and topics.

SESSION EVALUATION

On a 1 to 5 scale, rank the following about _(meeting session)_ . 5 = Excellent, 4 = Good, 3 = Average, 2 = Below Average, 1 = Poor.

____ Objectives clearly defined

____ Objectives met

____ Topic relevant to me

____ Time spent was

____ Speaker(s)

    ____ Organization of material

    ____ Delivery

    ____ Audio/visuals

    ____ Handouts

____ Audience interaction

____ Total Score

Suggestions for session topics for the next meeting _____

As participants fill out questionnaires evaluating the meeting, they can also supply the planner with profile information. The profile is used in many planning decisions such as program timing. This questionnaire can be designed where participants do a minimum of writing and so that computers can compile the information. The opportunity to survey attendees on specific subjects is presented. For example, the Teachers of Typing may be asked, "What text do you use for basic keyboarding?" The Maserati owners might be asked, "Where was your car purchased?" Use the basic profile questions. (See Chapter 2.)

PARTICIPANT PROFILE

Hometown Population

❑ Over 1,000,000   ❑ 100,000   ❑ 50,000   ❑ 25,000 or under

Distance from meeting city

❑ Under 100 miles   ❑ 100–300 miles

❑ 300–600 miles   ❑ Over 600 miles

Age

❑ Under 25   ❑ 25–35   ❑ 35–45   ❑ 45–55   ❑ Over 55

Sex

❑ Female   ❑ Male

Occupation _____

Type business

❑ Manufacturing   ❑ Distribution   ❑ Service   ❑ Government

Average Income

❑ Under $25,000   ❑ $25–35,000   ❑ $36–50,000   ❑ Over $50,000

Did a companion accompany you?   ❑ Yes   ❑ No

If so, age and sex

_____ Age   ❑ Female   ❑ Male

Means of payment for the meeting

❑ Self   ❑ Employer   ❑ Cash   ❑ Personal check   ❑ Credit card

Follow-Up

At the closing gavel, a meeting planner's job does not end. There are several follow-up activities that must be performed.

At the property, tips must be distributed. Note that a gratuity will have been added to many items, such as food and beverage service. It is up to the planner whether or not to supplement this. Service beyond what is usually expected should be rewarded.

The master account must be verified. During the meeting, the planner should review this daily. Individual room folios should be reviewed and a final count made of room nights used. If complimentary suites were included in the contract, be sure that the property did not charge for them inadvertently.

Shipments of materials must be inventoried and made. They should be inventoried again once they are delivered to the home office after the meeting.

Back at the office several follow-up activities occur. Statistics on how many people attended, how many meals were served, how many people used ground transportation, and how many tickets were sold should be compiled. The final attendee list should be updated.

If continuing education units are awarded, the certificates must be sent out to attendees who earned them.

If proceedings are to be distributed the mailing list should be confirmed and transcriptions edited, printed, and sent out.

Thank you letters should be sent to the property staff and to outside contractors that were helpful. Upper-level staff do not receive tips. Their rewards are thank you letters and recommendations to their employers.

The meeting planner should also meet with the meeting sponsor's management to give personal recommendations and evaluation. All suggestions for the next meeting should then be put in writing by the planner.

Travel reimbursements must be paid to staff and no-charge presentors, and contractors' bills must be paid. A final adjustment of the property master account should be made and payment sent. After all bills are paid, a final income/expense statement should be formulated and justified with the budget.

A sense of satisfaction can be enjoyed by the meeting planner when the last follow-up activity has been done. Looking back at the many decisions that were made and the minute details that were taken care of, the planner has a feeling of accomplishment. The puzzle came together piece by piece. The many parts fit to make a complete picture and a successful meeting was produced.

Budgeting

ne of the first questions that a meeting planner should be able to answer is "What is the meeting budget?" A *budget* is an estimation of costs and how they will be allocated.

The planner first determines who pays for the meeting. For many corporate and incentive meetings, the costs are paid by the meeting sponsor. When individuals are expected to pay for their own transportation, accommodations, and a registration fee, the meeting planner must work to keep the meeting costs affordable. The registration fee in particular is often closely correlated with the total meeting costs.

Budget projections are often derived from the records of past expenditures. If no similar meeting has been held previously, the planner or the organization's manager may develop a budget after researching the costs for program components such as speaker fees, accommodations, travel, and food and beverage service.

The goal in budgeting is to calculate correctly or to come in under budget. The planner must be aware of inflation, particularly when a meeting is projected and budgeted two or three years before it is to occur. Changing the meeting location, program content, and registration policies can be costly. Paying a speaker a $4,000 fee can destroy a budget. Using three breakout rooms instead of one general session room costs more. Allowing local attendees to attend sessions at a national meeting at no cost may take up space that otherwise could be sold.

If there is no past meeting history from which to derive a budget projection and the planner is given management's set dollar allocation for the event, or if the planner is asked to develop a budget, the following questions must be answered:

❑ **What are the objectives of the meeting?** Chapter 3 discusses meeting objectives such as education, internal business, motivation, and pleasure. Some organizations are willing to incur a monetary loss to achieve these objectives. But if the purpose of the meeting is to produce revenue, then budgeting has to be approached with the idea of keeping expenses as low as possible and setting registration and program fees that will not only cover expenses but also generate a profit.

❑ **How many people are expected to attend the meeting?** As with buying in quantity, holding a meeting for 200 is less expensive per person than holding a meeting for 20. The room that accommodates 20 is more expensive per person than one that seats 200. Many property charges are based on volume. If 300 are expected for a meeting, the property can count on booking and charging for several hundred sleeping rooms and serving 300 meals. Thus, it may lower its rates for function rooms.

❑ **Where is the meeting being held?** As explained in Chapter 4, some cities are more expensive than others. Some properties are more expensive than others. Sleeping room charges vary with each property. Factors such as the time of the year when the meeting is held and the cost of transportation to and from the meeting figure into budgeting.

❑ **Who pays? (individuals or organization)** If the organization holding the meeting pays for all expenses, then budgeting is simpler. The meeting planner may simply have a predetermined budget and will not have to keep track of participants' payments. Management decides on the meeting expenses. If individuals pay their own meeting expenses, unknown factors, primarily attendance figures, come into play.

❑ **For how many people will the meeting sponsor pay transportation, accommodations, and registration fees? How many room nights are involved?** This is less important for an incentive meeting where all attendees' expenses are paid. Where attendees pay their own registration fees speaker/staff costs, which are paid by all participants, must be taken into consideration. A meeting where 70 speakers are brought in, all expenses paid, is costly.

❑ **What are the program components?** Food and beverage service, paid speakers and entertainment, audiovisual requirements, off-site sessions, and hospitality all add costs to a meeting. Yet some of these costs are the most easily controlled. The planner can find sponsors to underwrite the costs of hospitality suites, a speaker may reduce his or her fee, and some audiovisual equipment can be borrowed instead of rented.

As with any budgeting, there are fixed and variable costs. If the exact number of attendees is unknown, almost all of the costs are variable, since they are based on the estimated number of people attending. For example, per person meal costs are set but the total budget for food and beverage service is inexact.

Sample Budget Exercise

The following problem illustrates how to prepare a meeting budget. A three-day, two-night national meeting is planned. From past meeting history, it is estimated that 200 people will attend. The objectives of the meeting are education and networking. It is not expected that the meeting will generate income. Participants will pay their own transportation, accommodations, and registration fees. Lunch will be served on all three days, and a banquet and reception will be held one evening. A four-hour sightseeing tour is scheduled. Several small exhibits will be set up in the registration area. There are five speakers and four staff members whose expenses will be paid.

Preparing the Expense Statement

❑ **Transportation.** List two cities that are very far from the meeting city and two that are within 200 miles. Ask a travel agent or airline for estimated air fares from those cities. Decide whether refundable or nonrefundable tickets will be purchased (see Chapter 12). Add the ticket prices together and divide by four to get an estimated per person estimated transportation cost. For the purposes of the sample problem, assume that this figure is

$335. Add in transfer (airport to hotel) costs. Multiply the total by how many people will have their own transportation paid. (More accurate figures can be used when speaker and staff transportation costs are calculated because one knows where these people are geographically located in relation to the meeting site.)

Average airfare:	$335 × 9 =	$ 3,015
Transfer costs:	$25 × 9 =	$ 225

Speaker/staff transportation

subtotal $ 3,240

❑ **Lodging.** Assume that the hotel will cost $75 per night plus $8.25 tax (unless tax exempt organization)

Two night's lodging: $75 × 9 = $ 1,499

❑ **Registration fees.** These fees are usually waived for speakers and staff, but they should be considered expenses because they cover items such as food and materials. For now the figure must be left blank. It can be inserted when the first registration fee is estimated. Take all other fees added and divide by 200. Assume that figure is $300.

Registration: 300 × 9 = $ 2,700

❑ **Function room rental.** See Chapter 5, which explains sliding costs of function rooms. Assume that 350 room nights will be used and that the property contract specifies that meeting room charges will be $5,000.

Function room rental: $ 5,000

❑ **Audiovisual equipment rental.** Assume that audiovisual equipment rental will cost $3,500.

A/V rental: $ 3,500

❑ **Speaker fees.** One speaker ($1,000 honorarium)

Speaker fee: $ 1,000

❑ **Speaker gifts/awards.** 5 plaques at $45 each and one award plaque at $60 + $14.25 tax

Gifts/awards: $ 299

❑ **Food and Beverage.** Expect that 200 people will eat lunch each day and that 175 people will attend the banquet. Drinks at the reception are $3 each; plan on two per person.

Lunch:	$19 + 5% tax + 18% gratuity =	
	$23 × 3 × 200 =	$13,000
Banquet:	$45 + $10 tax and gratuity =	
	$55 × 175 =	$ 9,625
Reception:	$3 × 2 × 175 plus 23% tax and	
	gratuity =	$ 1,292
Canapes:	$600 + $138 tax and gratuity =	$ 738
	Food and beverage subtotal	**$25,455**

❑ **Free Time/Transportation.** Buses rent for $250/hour, and the museum has an entry fee.

Buses:	$250 × 4 hrs. × 4 vehicles =	$ 4,000
Museum:	$5.50/person × 175 =	$ 963
	Free time/Transportation subtotal	**$ 4,963**

❑ **Personnel/Overhead.** The planner and one support staff handle four meetings per year.

One-fourth salary and benefits:		$11,253
One-fourth office rental and utilities:		$ 3,000
Overtime during the	3 staff × 4 hours × 3 days =	
meeting *(overtime*	36 hours × $16.50 =	$ 594
wage $16.50/hr.)		
	Plus $2.53 benefits/hour =	$ 91
Meeting planner's inspection tour =		$ 500
Staff lodging before		
meeting:	$83.25/night × 4 room nights =	$ 333
	Personnel Overhead subtotal	**$15,771**

❑ **Marketing.** The planner should figure the costs of marketing into the budget.

Brochure design:	$ 200
Brochure printing	
(1,000 copies; 2 sides; 1 color ink and paper):	$ 150
Brochure postage:	$ 250
Miscellaneous postage:	$ 100
Trade journal ad:	$ 450
News releases and postage:	$ 100
Marketing subtotal	**$ 1,250**

❑ **Materials.** The planner should add the cost of meeting materials to the budget.

8-page program (design and print):	$ 350
Nametags and holders:	$ 150
F&B and free-time tickets:	$ 100
Signs (3 × $60 plus tax):	$ 189
12-page attendee list:	$ 262
Flowers:	$ 293
Materials subtotal	$ 1,345

❑ **Miscellaneous.** Tips, insurance, incidentals.

Miscellaneous:	$ 1,000
Total	**$67,022**

(If the meeting is planned to be held in 12 months, then 5% per year should be added to these estimates to cover inflation.)

Divide $67,257 by 200 anticipated attendance for an estimated per person cost of $336.

Now look at income from sources other than registration fees:

Income Statement

Exhibitors:	4 at $500 each =	$2,000
Sponsor for one lunch =		$4,600
Interest:	Since many of the bills will not be due until after the meeting is over, registration fees can be placed in an interest-bearing account as they are received. Interest of 5% on an average of $30,000 for 6 months =	$ 750
Advertising in program:	5 ads at $175 =	$ 875
Registration:	10 1-day only at $100 each =	$1,000
	Total	**$9,225**

Calculating the Registration Fee and Total Income

To reach the registration fee, subtract income ($9,225) from expenses ($67,022) for a total ($57,797). Divide the total by the number of expected participants (200) for a registration fee ($289). Set the registration fee at $295 for registrations that are received six weeks before the meeting and $345 thereafter. (Remember that the earlier registration money earns interest.)

Now the total income can be calculated.

Miscellaneous =	$ 9,225
155 registrations @ $295 =	$45,725
45 registrations @ $345 =	$15,525
Total Income	$70,475

The difference between expected expenses and expected income is $3,453. This is roughly 5% which is a reasonable cushion to allow.

Monitoring the Budget

The budget should be reviewed at least monthly. During the three months prior to the meeting, it should be reviewed weekly.

Accounting can be done on either a cash or an accrual basis. With a cash basis, funds are deleted when paid and added when received. On an accrual basis, income is accountable when due and expenses are deducted when due, though money may not actually have been received or sent.

An accounts receivable ledger may be needed when purchase orders, partial payments, and underpayment are issues. If there is a date on which the registration fee rises, those who do not make the deadline have to be billed.

Establishing credit with the meeting property is usually initiated by submitting a credit approval form. If credit is denied, then the property will require a deposit, often the full amount expected to be spent. A meal, once served, cannot be returned. The time that a meeting room is used is gone.

The meeting planner should review the master hotel account daily. The account will reflect guest room charges and catering fees. Function room charges and audiovisual equipment charges may be entered on the master account daily, but they are not usually added in until the last day.

Speakers and staff members whose expenses were covered will be sending in travel reimbursement forms. Checking accounts must be kept open for some months after the meeting to make these payments.

Estimating a meeting will cost $70,000 and in the final accounting seeing that the meeting cost $69,500 gives a meeting planner a huge sense of achievement. Accurate budgeting and keeping precise records is an important part of the planner's duties and separates the professional from the amateur.

Index

A

B

C

D

F

RI